Bangladesh

Frontispiece: **Rickshaws**

Consultant: Flora Halim Chowdhury, Associate Professor & Chair, Women's, Gender, and Sexuality Studies Department, University of Massachusetts Boston

Please note: All statistics are as up-to-date as possible at the time of publication.

Book production by The Design Lab

Library of Congress Cataloging-in-Publication Data
Names: Orr, Tamra, author.
Title: Bangladesh / by Tamra B. Orr.
Description: New York : Children's Press, an imprint of Scholastic Inc., 2019. | Series:
     Enchantment of the world | Includes bibliographical references and index.
Identifiers: LCCN 2017057578 | ISBN 9780531130506 (library binding)
Subjects: LCSH: Bangladesh—Juvenile literature.
Classification: LCC DS393.4 .O77 2019 | DDC 954.92—dc23
LC record available at https://lccn.loc.gov/2017057578

Scholastic Inc., 557 Broadway, New York, NY 10012

1 2 3 4 5 6 7 8 9 10 R 28 27 26 25 24 23 22 21 20 19

Bangladesh

BY TAMRA B. ORR

Enchantment of the World™
Second Series

CHILDREN'S PRESS®

An Imprint of Scholastic Inc.

Contents

Left to right: **Reading the Qur'an, printing on fabric, glory lily, collecting water lilies, girls**

CHAPTER I

Land of the Bengals

VISIT BANGLADESH AND WHAT DO YOU SEE? WATER. There is water everywhere you turn in this South Asian nation, with thousands of miles of coastline and countless rivers and wetlands. Bangladesh is home to thick mangrove swamps, where the majestic Bengal tiger lives.

It is also home to millions of warm and welcoming people. With about 165 million people, Bangladesh is one of the most populated countries in the world. As a relatively small country, this makes it one of the most densely populated regions on earth.

Historically, Bangladesh belonged to a region called Bengal, which was part of India. For a time, India was a colony of Great Britain. In 1947, India became independent. It was immediately partitioned, becoming two countries—India and Pakistan. The people of India were primarily Hindu, and those from Pakistan were primarily Muslim. Pakistan itself was made

Opposite: **Women carry loads of tea leaves after harvesting them. Nearly half of all Bangladeshis work in agriculture.**

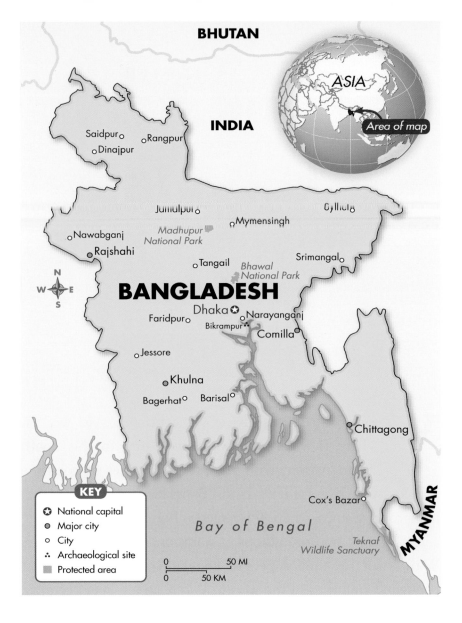

KEY

⊛ National capital
● Major city
○ City
∴ Archaeological site
▪ Protected area

0   50 MI
0   50 KM

up of two parts. In 1971, the eastern part became the nation of Bangladesh, which means "Land of the Bengals."

Today, the people of Bangladesh face many challenges. Their low-lying land frequently floods, and as global climate change causes sea levels to rise, this will only get worse. The country also has a large, relatively poor population.

But some things are improving. People have greater access to health care and education. Population growth is slowing as families are having fewer children. The economy is expanding. In particular, the garment industry has grown dramatically in recent years. New programs are also creating better and safer work conditions for Bangladeshis. In these and many other ways, Bangladesh is becoming a stronger nation. Come explore Bangladesh.

Bangladeshi girls in their school uniforms walk home after school. Boys and girls now attend school in equal numbers in Bangladesh.

CHAPTER 2

A Land under Threat

THE OLD SAYING THAT "GOOD THINGS COME IN SMALL packages" rings true when exploring Bangladesh. It is a small country, only a little bigger than the size of the U.S. state of Iowa.

India surrounds most of Bangladesh. In the southeast, Bangladesh shares a short border with Myanmar. The Bay of Bengal, an arm of the Indian Ocean, lies to the south.

Opposite: **Most of the land in Bangladesh is low and flat.**

Plains and Hills

Almost all of Bangladesh is made up of alluvial soil. Alluvial soil is full of minerals left over from the constant flooding of rivers and the dirt and sand they leave behind. This makes the land very fertile. The rich soil is what attracted the country's first settlers long ago and why, throughout Bangladesh's history, much of the economy has centered on agriculture.

Traditional fishing boats are moored along the beach at Cox's Bazar.

Cox's Bazar

In 1798, Hiram Cox, a young Scottish captain, was sent to what is now Myanmar as a representative of the East India Company. While there, he ventured out to Ramu in present-day Bangladesh. His main purpose was to set up marketplaces for trading between the two countries. Little is known about what Cox achieved while he was there, but following his death in 1799, the biggest marketplace was named after him. Today Cox's Bazar is a popular resort, with many tourists visiting to enjoy its long beach and endless rows of shops.

Alluvial plains make up the majority of the land in Bangladesh. These areas are quite flat, and most are only about 50 feet (15 meters) above sea level. This makes them especially vulnerable to flooding. Several large cities and thousands of small villages are located on Bangladesh's alluvial plains. A city called Cox's Bazar lies in the country's southeast corner. It has the world's largest stretch of uninter-rupted natural beach, stretching 62.5 miles (100 kilometers).

The only hills in the country are found in the Sylhet region of the northeast and the Chittagong region of the southeast. This is where tea plantations and rain forests are located. The country's highest peak, Mount Keokradong, is in the Chittagong Hills. It rises 4,035 feet (1,230 m) above sea level.

The Chittagong region contains rugged mountains covered with thick forests.

Bangladesh's Geographic Features

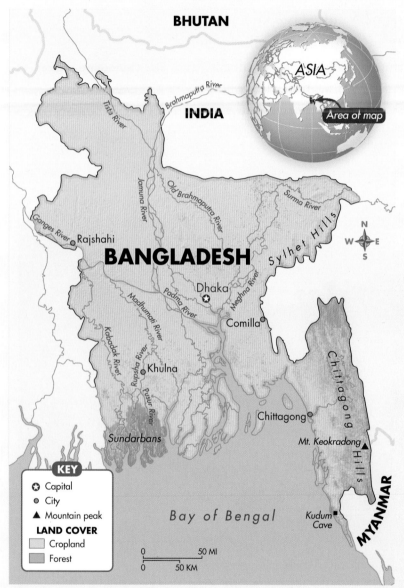

Area: 57,320 square miles (148,460 sq km)

Greatest Distance East to West: 410 miles (660 km)

Greatest Distance North to South: 509 miles (820 km)

Longest Shared Border: With India, 2,545 miles (4,096 km)

Length of Coastline: 223 miles (359 km)

Highest Elevation: Mount Keokradong, 4,035 feet (1,230 m)

Lowest Elevation: Sea level along the coast

Average Daily High Temperature: In Dhaka, 91°F (33°C) in June, 80°F (27°C) in December

Average Daily Low Temperature: In Dhaka, 80°F (27°C) in June, 57°F (14°C) in December

Average Annual Precipitation: In Dhaka, 85 inches (216 cm)

A Watery World

Look at Bangladesh from an aerial photo and it's apparent how much water dominates the country. About 5,000 miles (8,000 km) of waterways flow through Bangladesh. There are hundreds of rivers, lakes, swamps, and marshes. The nation's three primary rivers are the Brahmaputra, the Ganges, and the Meghna. Water from these rivers is used for everything from traveling and irrigating fields to drinking and bathing. Bangladesh's waterways change in size and flow, based on the country's weather. During the rainy season, rivers overflow and spill across the land. If the rainfall is too heavy and the flooding too serious, crops can be ruined and nothing can grow.

In many parts of Bangladesh, houses are built on stilts to protect them from floods.

Island Life

When the rainy season ends and the land begins to dry out, some people move onto a piece of land called a char. A char is a raised area much like a sandbar. Sometimes it is attached to the mainland, but more often chars are islands in the middle of rivers.

Because Bangladesh is one of the most crowded countries in the world, finding a place to build a home and live can be difficult. Some people settle on chars, but it is risky. When the water rises or a storm blows in, erosion eats away at the soil, and the small islands are threatened. The people living on chars do what they can to protect their homes from nature. They plant trees and bushes to push back the water, but it is often a losing battle. "It is the natural process," said Abdul Motalib, a young man who was born on a char more than twenty-five years ago and has moved from one char to another his entire life. "If this char washes away, we will look for another one. That is our destiny." Chars have no schools, no doctors, no police officers, and no businesses. People survive on them as long as they can, until it is clear the land is going to be submerged. Then they pack up and move on.

In southwestern Bangladesh is a unique region called the Sundarbans. The word *Sundarbans* means "beautiful forest," and this region lives up to its name. It includes the world's largest mangrove forest. Mangroves are trees that can grow in salt water. Mangroves are multitasking trees: They buffer the water washing up against the shore, keeping it from eroding. They provide important habitat for fish and other wildlife. On top of that, many Bangladeshis use their wood for timber and their leaves to weave roofs for homes.

An elevated pathway leads through the forest in the Sundarbans, so that visitors can explore when the area is flooded.

Urban Landscapes

Dhaka, the capital of Bangladesh, is the country's largest city, home to more than ten million people. The second-largest city in Bangladesh is Chittagong. It is home to almost four million people and is one of the fastest growing cities in the country. Over the years, Chittagong has been an important port, a military base, and the center of Bangladesh's fight for independence. The city has a mixed population with people of many different ethnic and religious groups living there. It is filled with mosques and shrines.

Khulna, home to 1.3 million people, is the nation's third-largest city. It lies in the southwest along the Rupsha River. Many companies are headquartered in this city, as is the Bangladesh navy. The area is known as the Gateway to the

The city of Khulna is growing quickly.

Sundarbans, with many steamboats leaving the port to visit the mangrove forest there.

Rajshahi, a city along the Padma River in the west, has a population of more than 700,000, making it the nation's fourth-largest city. Rajshahi dates back to the early seventeenth century. Today, it is known for its silk production. It is also a center for commerce and education.

The fifth-largest city in Bangladesh is Comilla, which lies in the southeast. Nearly 400,000 people live there. One of the country's oldest cities, today it is home to many jute and cotton mills. The city is filled with reservoirs, some of which were built more than five hundred years ago.

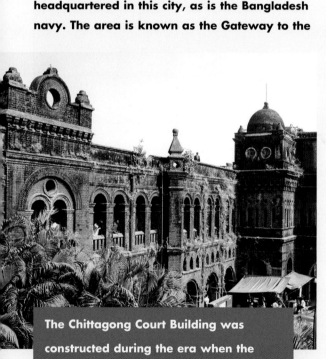

The Chittagong Court Building was constructed during the era when the British ruled the region.

Dangerous Air and Water

One of the growing problems faced in Bangladesh's biggest cities is air pollution. In 2017, the World Health Organization (WHO) ranked Bangladesh as fourth among ninety-one countries for worst air quality. The capital city of Dhaka has some of the worst pollution in the world. Major sources of the pollution include thousands of poorly maintained vehicles and particles from construction. According to WHO, air pollution is responsible for the death of 280,000 children in Bangladesh each year. Even the air inside houses is often polluted because people burn firewood to cook, creating smoky rooms.

Water pollution is also a problem for the people of Bangladesh. In the past, UNICEF, an international organization that focuses on improving children's health, tried to

Pollution in Bangladesh is sometimes so bad that the air looks brown. Brick-making factories fueled by coal and wood are a major source of air pollution.

A boy drinks from a well in Bangladesh.

help solve the pollution problem by digging millions of wells. However, it quickly became clear that Bangladesh's soil was contaminated with arsenic, a lethal chemical. In addition, rivers and other waterways are contaminated with human waste and polluted industrial runoff.

Three Seasons

Bangladesh has three seasons. Winter lasts from October to March, and summer from March to June. June to October is called monsoon season. Summers are hot and humid, with the frequent threat of thunderstorms, sometimes with hail. Winters are a little cooler, but the temperatures still often hit 80 degrees Fahrenheit (27 degrees Celsius).

Monsoon season is the most challenging time of year. Rain falls constantly, with the western part of the country getting about 55 inches (140 centimeters) a year, and the northeast an astounding 235 inches (600 cm)! The rainfall makes life much more difficult, especially when there are cyclones. These storms form over the ocean and bring high winds, and strong water surges that force rivers to swell and overflow their banks. Crops are flooded, and people scramble to cope with the weather until the season changes again.

Boys leap into a river on a hot day in Dhaka. The average high temperature in the city is above 90°F (32°C) eight months of the year.

Monstrous Monsoons

In Bangladesh, the rainy season earns its name. More than three-quarters of the country's annual rainfall occurs during monsoon season, between the months of June and October. By the time it is over, typically one-third of the country is underwater. Many neighborhoods can be reached only by boat. Every year, houses are damaged or destroyed. Crops are flooded and livestock drowned. Schools close. Countless people die during the storm season. The year 2017 had an especially brutal monsoon season. Hundreds of thousands of homes were ruined and 140 people died in the high waters.

The Dangers of Rising Seas

Since the industrial revolution of about two hundred years ago, humans have burnt huge quantities of coal and oil to power factories and cars. This has sent massive amounts of pollutants into the air, which has changed the climate. The average temperature around the globe is increasing. Much of

Meandering rivers run through much of the land in Bangladesh.

the world's water is frozen in the polar ice caps, but as temperatures increase, some of this ice is melting, causing sea levels to rise.

Of all the countries in the world, Bangladesh is the one most at risk from climate change. It is a low-lying country situated on the planet's largest river delta, which is formed by the junction of the Brahmaputra, Ganges, and Meghna Rivers. The country has more than 230 major rivers and streams.

One-quarter of Bangladesh is less than 7 feet (2 m) above sea level. Two-thirds of it is less than 15 feet (4 m) above sea level. As the oceans rise, many Bangladeshis' homes will be flooded. People will be forced to move inland and rebuild, if they can find the room.

The rising temperatures also change weather patterns, causing an increase in severe storms. In 2016, four cyclones

During severe floods, as much as three-quarters of the land in Bangladesh is inundated.

hit the country. The storms have become more intense as well. The storms barreling in off the ocean create huge waves called storm surges. The storm surges from recent cyclones have pushed water 50 to 60 miles (80 to 95 km) up the country's rivers. Not only does this flood crops, but the salty water damages the soil and contaminates freshwater supplies. Food shortages, already a problem in Bangladesh, have increased. In some places, embankments have been built to try to protect the land from the salt water, but they frequently break.

Some experts predict that unless major changes are made by the year 2100, sea levels may rise as much as 6 feet (1.8 m). But even a 3-foot (1 m) rise in sea level would submerge 20 percent of Bangladesh. More than thirty million people would lose their homes and land. A rise of 6 feet (1.8 m) would displace fifty million people.

Combating Climate Change

Bangladesh currently spends about $1 billion to try to protect its people and land from the effects of climate change. It has implemented an early warning system to alert people to approaching cyclones. It has built 2,100 cyclone shelters capable of holding more than a million people. More than

Many sturdy, elevated cyclone shelters have been built in Bangladesh, so people can be safe during storms and floods.

4,000 miles (6,400 km) of coastal area have embankment projects in the works. People are planting trees on some of the most threatened islands, because trees, especially mangroves, help protect the land against storm surges. In addition, some companies are working to develop salt-resistant rice that can grow when covered with salt water.

Although Bangladesh has produced little of the pollutants that have caused climate change, it is paying a heavier price

Workers repair an embankment in Bangladesh. Rising seas threaten millions of Bangladeshis.

than almost any other country. Many people believe that other countries—especially those that generated most of the pollutants—should help Bangladesh deal with the effects of rising seas and the huge number of people who will be forced to move. According to Atiq Rahman, executive director of the Bangladesh Center for Advanced Studies, "It's a matter of global justice." Tariq Karim, Bangladesh's ambassador to India, has said, "We need a regional and, better yet, a global solution. And if we don't get one soon, the Bangladeshi people will soon become the world's problem, because we will not be able to keep them."

Rising seas and increasingly severe storms have destroyed the homes and farms of many people along the coast of Bangladesh. This has prompted many rural Bangladeshis to abandon their villages and move to Dhaka, where they hope to find a better life.

CHAPTER 3

The Natural World

WHEN YOU MIX RICH SOIL WITH PLENTY OF RAIN and sunshine, you get a land bursting with colorful flowers, lush forests, and varied animal life. This is Bangladesh.

Trees and Bamboo

About 15 percent of Bangladesh is covered in forest. Many types of trees grow there. Some of the most common are the date palm and the coconut palm. The babul, a thorny tree in the acacia family, thrives in the plains. Mangrove trees, which are unusual because they can grow up out of salt water, are found in the Sundarbans, along the Bay of Bengal. Teak also grows in the Sundarbans. Bamboo, which is a type of grass common in Bangladesh, grows as tall as trees and is often used to make paper.

Opposite: **Ratargul Swamp Forest is the only freshwater swamp in Bangladesh. Much of the forest is underwater throughout the year. In the rainy season, the water can get as deep as 30 feet (9 m).**

An Oily Nightmare

In 2014, the *Southern Star 7*, a tanker loaded with 92,000 gallons (350,000 liters) of oil, was docked near Mrigamari, where the Sela and Pusur Rivers join. Suddenly, on the morning of December 9, a cargo vessel appeared out of the fog. Nothing could be done to stop the collision between the two ships. Soon oil was rushing into the water.

The oil spilled and spread. It covered 40 miles (65 km) along the Sela and Pusur Rivers. It devastated this area, which is at the entrance to the Sundarbans, the country's huge mangrove forest. Dolphins, otters, egrets, crocodiles, and many more creatures were covered with oil. It was not long before villagers and fishers were talking about the

Bangladeshis wade into the water to collect oil that has spread across it.

A Bangladeshi washes a kingfisher bird to remove oil from its feathers.

smell of the oil and the sight of dead fish and other water creatures.

Local residents joined the effort to clean up the oil. Men, women, and children waded out into the water, and, with their bare hands, scraped the thick, black goop from reeds, leaves, and tree trunks and into large cooking pots or their boats. It was a slow, tedious, dirty process, but they needed to help save the nature where they live. Oil can suffocate the roots of the mangroves, killing the trees and the creatures large and small that live in the forest.

A walk through any of Bangladesh's fruit markets is enough to make anyone hungry. Every city has markets with rows and rows of stalls. They feature boxes, bowls, and other containers overflowing with brightly colored fruit of every shape and size. Many of these fruits are familiar to North Americans. Apples, grapes, figs, and bananas hang overhead, while just below there are samples of pineapple and watermelon. Next to them, shoppers can choose from many different varieties

Jackfruit is the world's largest tree fruit. Some weigh as much as 110 pounds (50 kilograms).

The National Flower

Bangladesh's national flower is the *shapla*, or water lily. It has bright pink or white petals. During the warmest months of the year, it can be seen floating on the country's many waterways. Bangladeshis boil or roast the plant's roots to eat them. The flower and leaves are also edible. In addition, the water lily has been used in medicines to treat stomach ailments and other health problems.

Bangladeshis collect water lilies from a lake. They bring the flowers to market to sell as food.

of mango. Customers might also purchase litchi, star fruit, or coconut while there, or take home the country's national fruit, the jackfruit. Bursting with hundreds of seeds, the green fuzzy jackfruit is huge. It tastes something like a blend of banana and pineapple. Its seeds are delicious when roasted or fried.

Many fruits are also sold at floating markets. Vendors paddle down waterways, selling fruits from their boats.

Bursts of Color

Flowers abound throughout Bangladesh. Water lilies decorate the marshes in bursts of white and pink. Krishnachura trees burst into color in the summer with bright red flowers. Festivals are held in some cities at the beginning of May to celebrate these blossoms. Everyone knows when the *beli*, or jasmine flowers, bloom. The smell is powerful and entrancing. Bright orange marigolds grow in the winter. Their leaves are sometimes used to treat open wounds or other injuries.

Wonderful Wildlife

The people of Bangladesh share their land with hundreds of different species of mammals, reptiles, and amphibians. But some of these animals are in danger. A number of species have been threatened by a combination of deforestation, loss of habitat, and illegal hunting. Animals that are no longer found in Bangladesh include marsh crocodiles, gray wolves, swamp deer, and blackbuck antelopes. Today, about two hundred species are considered threatened, including wild elephants, which live in the Chittagong Hills.

Gharials, one of the world's most endangered species, live in the rivers of Bangladesh and other South Asian nations. They have 110 teeth, which they use to catch fish.

A royal Bengal tiger prowls through the grass in Bangladesh.

Dwindling Hope for Tigers

The boldly striped royal Bengal tiger is Bangladesh's national animal. Males grow more than 10 feet (3 m) long and weigh hundreds of pounds. A century ago, forty thousand of these tigers lived throughout Asia. By the 1970s, that number had dropped to two thousand. The creatures were hunted for their richly colored fur. In addition, various tiger body parts are used in herbal medicines, because they are thought to cure everything from cancer to baldness. As more people move into the cats' natural habitats, interactions between humans and tigers have increased. Tigers have sometimes killed humans. People from the Sundarbans and mangrove forests where the tigers live have to keep an eye out constantly for that sudden flash of orange and black that means danger.

Today, probably only about one hundred Bengal tigers live in Bangladesh. To determine exactly how many tigers are left in the area, wildlife experts have installed more than eight hundred cameras in about four hundred different stations to keep track of tiger movement. When the photos are analyzed, experts will have a good idea of the number of tigers in Bangladesh. Hopefully, the population of these noble creatures will not be as low as some fear.

Many types of apes and monkeys live in the Sundarbans region of the Bangladesh. The most common type of monkey in Bangladesh is the rhesus macaque. It is highly adaptable, living in forests, open areas, and cities. Another type of monkey found in Bangladesh is the pig-tailed macaque. It gets its name from its short tail, which has little or no hair. Pig-tailed macaques are found in the country's northeastern and southeastern forests. The unusual hoolock gibbon defends its territory by whistling loud songs, earning it the nickname "the singing ape."

Hanuman langurs live in western Bangladesh. Black when they are born, they turn gray or tan as adults.

Forest reaches the beach along the Bay of Bengal at Teknaf Wildlife Sanctuary.

Places of Protection

The government of Bangladesh is working to protect the nation's wildlife. The country now has eight national parks, seven wildlife sanctuaries, five conservation sites, and one game reserve. These spots help protect the nation's remaining Bengal tigers, wild elephants, and clouded leopards.

The Teknaf Wildlife Sanctuary, at the country's southernmost tip, is a good place to see Bangladesh nature up close. It features hiking trails through thick forests filled with bamboo. Many visitors stop by the Kudum Cave, nicknamed the Bat Cave. It is home to two species of bats, as well as many types of snails, spiders, and fish.

Madhupur National Park includes beautiful forests and swift streams. It provides habitat for monkeys, deer, and many birds. Another forested park, Bhawal National Park, is home to crocodiles, monkeys, foxes, and many other creatures. Despite being protected areas, the forests in both of these parks are shrinking as people cut the trees for timber.

The spectacular glory lily grows in Madhupur National Park.

Bangladesh is home to two types of bears: the Asiatic black bear and the sun bear. The forests are also home to tiny muntjac deer and large sambar deer.

Jackals fill the air with the sound of their howling at night. Jackals, which are related to wolves, are omnivores, meaning they eat all kinds of food. They prey on rodents and reptiles but also eat fruit and scavenge through garbage looking for scraps.

Many sea creatures live in Bangladesh's coastal waters. Whales, sharks, and sea turtles all swim in the Bay of Bengal. The area near the Sundarbans is particularly rich in dolphins. Eleven different dolphin species have been discovered there.

Groups of chital, also known as spotted deer, dine on mangroves in the Sundarbans.

Birds

Bird-watchers consider Bangladesh one of the best spots in the world to bring their binoculars. Along with the almost 400 types of birds that live in the country, an additional 240 species of migrating birds stop in Bangladesh on their journeys. Flamingos, which have long legs and pink feathers, can often be seen feeding in the shallow waters in the eastern part of the country. Nightjars live throughout Bangladesh. As their name implies, they usually come out at night to hunt for food. They build their nests on the ground, and their mottled coloring helps them blend in with the leaves and bark in the forest.

Hoopoes are one of the many kinds of birds that live in Bangladesh. Their crown of feathers makes them easy to identify.

Insects

Many thousands of kinds of insects live in Bangladesh. These include beautiful butterflies and buzzing bees.

Some insects in Bangladesh are a problem. Mosquitoes, for example, breed well in standing water, so Bangladesh is a haven for them. Their bites can be annoyingly itchy, but mosquitoes can also be dangerous because they can carry and transmit deadly diseases such as malaria.

Other insects, such as crickets, grasshoppers, and ants, are an important source of food for people in Bangladesh. Currently, Bangladesh is one of the top ten countries where insects are a common part of the diet. Though eating insects has not caught on in the United States, it is common in many countries, and it is easy to see why: Insects are cheap, plentiful, and nutritious. Fried crickets, for example, have almost twice as much iron as steak.

A Bangladeshi woman arranges a net around her baby to provide protection against the bites of mosquitoes.

CHAPTER 4

From Empires to Independence

A T FIRST GLANCE, THE HISTORY OF BANGLADESH can seem short. The nation only achieved independence in 1971. People have lived in the area, however, for many thousands of years. A group called the Bang moved into the region as far back as 1000 BCE. Historians suspect they were people of varied heritage who were driven out of lands to the north, including Mongolia and India. The Bang people developed arts, trade, and agriculture.

Opposite: **The Hindu goddess Durga kills a buffalo in a sculpture from the twelfth century, during the Pala dynasty.**

Empires Rise and Fall

The first significant empire to spread across what are now India, Pakistan, and Bangladesh was the Mauryan Empire, which arose around 320 BCE. The best-known Mauryan leader was Asoka, who ruled in the third century BCE. During his reign, the Buddhist religion came to the region. Asoka's son,

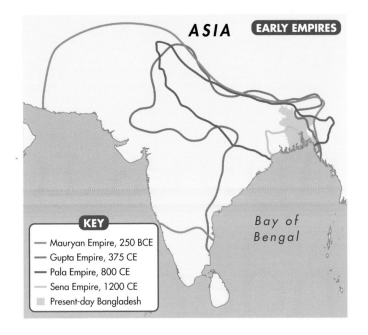

Mahinda, went to nearby Sri Lanka to spread the word about this new belief system.

The Mauryan Empire was replaced by the Gupta dynasty in the fourth century CE. The Guptas were Hindu. Although Hinduism grew in Bengal, the region that is now Bangladesh and the nearby part of India, Buddhism also remained. Hinduism and Buddhism were also practiced side by side during the Pala dynasty, which began in the eighth century CE. The Pala leaders were Buddhist, and Buddhism spread farther during their reign.

The Pala dynasty lasted four centuries until it was replaced by the Sena dynasty in 1150. The Senas were strong believers in Hinduism. Under their control, Buddhist ideas were pushed aside and Hindu beliefs were followed instead. In Bengal, many people who did not want to follow Hinduism fled to the Chittagong area.

Muslims Arrive

A few Muslims began arriving in Bengal during the twelfth century. In the early 1200s, Muhammad Bakhtiyar Khilji and his troops arrived from the north. They overthrew the Senas, captured Bengal, and brought it under Muslim control.

In the centuries that followed, Bengal flourished. Cities sprang up, palaces, forts, and mosques were built, roads and

Archaeologists carefully clean an artifact discovered at Bikrampur.

An Ancient Buddhist Temple

In early 2015, a team of researchers from Bangladesh and China made an exciting discovery in the city of Bikrampur. Under 23 feet (7 m) of dirt and rocks, they found the remains of a Buddhist temple that had been built more than a thousand years ago. They believe it is the site where Buddhist scholar and philosopher Atish Dipankar (980-1053) spent his early years. It is one of the oldest archaeological sites in all of Bangladesh.

Excavation on the site has unearthed an ancient city in addition to the temple. Diggers have found a number of stupas, dome-shaped mounds or shrines that often contain important Buddhist artifacts. A 10-foot (3 m) wall was also discovered. Traces of brick roads, as well as pottery items and ash pits, tell researchers that this area was once very busy. Each artifact the team finds provides another glimpse into life long, long ago.

bridges were constructed, and trade routes expanded. In 1576, the region officially joined the Mughal Empire. This empire covered most of what are now India, Pakistan, and Afghanistan. The city of Dhaka, now Bangladesh's capital, was established in 1608.

Lalbagh Fort was built in Dhaka during the Mughal period. Mughal buildings often feature arched doorways and many domes.

During the period of Muslim rule, Islam spread among people at all levels of society. But many people continued to practice Hinduism. Other people became Muslim but continued to incorporate aspects of Hinduism in their lives.

British Control

In the late seventeenth century, a Mughal emperor decided to sell three local villages to the British East India Company. Europeans had been coming to the area since the 1400s. The Portuguese, Dutch, British, and French had vied for power, but in the end it was the British who gained control.

The British East India Company had been established in 1600 in Great Britain. Its mission was to develop trade with India and East Asia. Once it owned three villages, the company began pushing for more and more territories and soon became dominant in the region.

The British presence brought some benefits to what is now Bangladesh. For example, they improved the region's infrastructure by building railroads. But they also introduced a feudal system under which landowners, called zamindars, were given tremendous power over poor peasant workers. In

Siraj al-Dawlah was the last leader of Bengal before the British East India Company gained control of the region.

Indian soldiers who worked for the British were called sepoys, from a term for "soldier" during the Mughal period. Today, the lowest ranked soldiers in the Bangladeshi army are called sepoys.

addition, under British rule, religious differences grew steadily. The Hindus in Bengal tended to cooperate with English rule. Most lived in the western part of the region. Muslims were more likely to fight the English. They mostly lived on farms in the east.

The British East India Company became so powerful it dictated laws and military decisions. The British altered the curriculum in schools so that the English language and culture were taught.

It was not long before the people began protesting at these unwanted changes. In 1857, they rebelled in what is known as the Sepoy Mutiny, or the First War of Independence. Although the British East India Company won the battle, it was forced to hand over control of the region to the British government. India, including what is now Bangladesh, was now a crown colony.

Toward Independence

For two centuries, the British maintained control of India, but the Bengal region in particular was difficult to administer. In 1905, the British officially divided Bengal into two parts. East Bengal, a Muslim region, had Dhaka as its capital, while West Bengal, a

Hindu region, had its capital in Calcutta (now Kolkata). This division was not acceptable to many Hindus in the west because they felt it would lessen their power. Muslims in the east were more likely to approve of the partition. Although the two parts of Bengal were reunited in 1912, the partition had increased hostility between Muslims and Hindus. Each group believed that the other was being favored.

In the following decades, Indians began calling for

Indian soldiers fight English troops during the Sepoy Mutiny, which began in Bengal.

self-rule. Hindus and Muslims realized that they would have to work together to achieve independence. Although tensions remained, groups such as the Muslim Khilafat movement joined the Congress Party, which was led by Hindus, in mass nonviolent protest.

Britain was slow to relinquish control, however. Over time, the British gave more Indians the right to vote and they placed more power in the hands of the governments of the Indian provinces. Finally, after continued protests and the turmoil of World War II, India became independent in 1947. Its long colonial era had come to an end.

Mahatma Gandhi (front, center) led the movement against British rule in India.

Hindus in East Pakistan crowd onto a train heading to India in 1947, following the partition of India.

Partition

As part of the end of colonial rule in 1947, Britain partitioned India, creating two countries. These countries were intended to be divided along religious lines, with Muslims living in Pakistan and Hindus in India. But in fact, both Muslims and Hindus lived in both countries.

In the months after partition, millions of people traveled from one country to the other to settle among people of the same religion. By 1948, fifteen million people had moved. It was the world's largest migration across borders. Many other people chose not to move. Today, India has one of the world's largest Muslim populations.

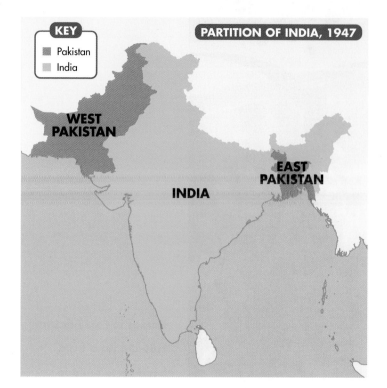

PARTITION OF INDIA, 1947

Pakistan
India

WEST
PAKISTAN

EAST
PAKISTAN

INDIA

East and West Pakistan

Pakistan itself was divided into two parts. West Pakistan was northwest of India. East Pakistan was east of India. The two parts of the country were separated by about 1,000 miles (1,600 km) of Indian territory.

The two parts of Pakistan were very different. West Pakistan was home to the country's government, businesses, and military, and the government was dominated by people from the west. East Pakistan was where most of the people lived. Many had little income since the majority of the country's revenue stayed in West Pakistan. East Pakistan was also more ethnically and religiously diverse than the western section.

In the 1950s, East Pakistan gained greater representation in the government. But government money was funneled into West Pakistan, even though East Pakistan produced more revenue. The people of East Pakistan also continued to suffer discrimination, and Bengalis were less likely to be given government jobs.

In 1970, a huge cyclone and tsunami, or great ocean wave, struck East Pakistan. More than half a million people were killed. The people of East Pakistan believed the government responded poorly to the disaster.

Every year on Martyrs' Day, Bangladeshis use flowers to decorate the monument in Dhaka honoring the martyrs of the language movement.

A War of Words

Another divisive issue in Pakistan was language. Many different languages are spoken in Pakistan. Government leaders thought having a common language would help unite the people of Pakistan. The Urdu language was chosen, even though only a small fraction of Pakistani people knew how to speak it. The people in East Pakistan wanted their commonly used Bengali language to be an official language. When Urdu was declared the country's sole official language, riots began in East Pakistan. Several students were shot at a demonstration in Dhaka on February 21, 1952.

Government officials then realized they had to compromise on the language issue. The government declared the two languages equal. To honor this decision and those who gave up their lives for it, February 21 is now known in Bangladesh as Martyrs' Day or Language Movement Day.

Discontent was rising. The people of East Pakistan saw themselves as completely distinct from those of West Pakistan.

The Bangladesh Liberation War

In December 1970, elections were held in Pakistan. The Awami League, a Muslim party in East Pakistan, won a majority of seats in the National Assembly. Sheikh Mujibur Rahman was the leader of the Awami League. He wanted greater autonomy, or self-government, for East Pakistan. As the leader of the party with the most seats in the National Assembly, Rahman should have become prime minister, the head of the government.

But Pakistani president Yahya Khan did not allow the newly elected National Assembly to meet. He sent the military

East Pakistani soldiers, police officers, and other volunteers joined together to fight for Bangladeshi independence.

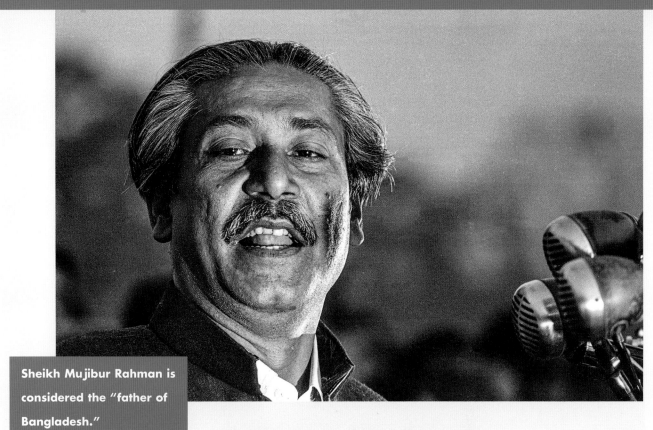

Sheikh Mujibur Rahman is considered the "father of Bangladesh."

A Memorable Speech

On March 7, 1970, Sheikh Mujibur Rahman made an important speech to the people about the prospect of independence. Rahman opened the speech with the words,

"Brothers of mine; Today I appear before you with a heavy heart. You know and understand everything. We tried with our lives. But the painful matter is that now the streets of Dhaka, Chittagong, Khulna, Rajshahi, and Rangpur are stained with the bloods of my brothers. Now the people of Bangla want freedom. The people of Bangla want to live. The people of Bangla want to have their rights. What wrong did we commit?"

In his speech, Rahman called for drastic changes for East Pakistan, including the end of martial law, the withdrawal of the military, and giving government power to the Bengali people. He ended the historic speech by saying, "Do not make this country a hell and destroy it." He continued,

"If we can solve things in a peaceful manner, we can at least live as brothers. Bear in mind that since we have given blood, we will give more. By the grace of Allah, we will surely liberate the people of this country. The struggle this time is the struggle for our emancipation. The struggle this time is the struggle for our independence. Joy Bangla."

into East Pakistan to arrest Rahman. A civil war began.

On March 26, 1971, East Pakistan declared its independence when one of the resistance leaders, Major Zia ur-Rahman, captured a radio station in Chittagong and called upon his people to rise up against West Pakistan.

The brutal Liberation War lasted nine months. The Pakistani army wanted to crush the Bengali independence movement. In an effort called Operation Searchlight, the army attacked the University of Dhaka and systematically slaughtered students. The military shelled residential neighborhoods and shot people in the streets. Millions of people, mostly Hindus, fled to India to escape the terror.

Students at the University of Dhaka light candles in memory of those killed in Operation Searchlight.

Many countries took sides in the conflict. The United States was an ally of Pakistan and wanted it to remain united. U.S. Navy ships entered the Bay of Bengal in support of Pakistan but did not get involved. India had a more direct interest in the war. Indira Gandhi, India's prime minister, decided it would be better to fight Pakistan than have to deal with an ever-growing flood of refugees. She ordered the Indian army into Pakistan to support the fight for Bengali independence. In December 1971, Pakistan gave up the fight. By that time, more than three million people had lost their lives. But Bangladesh had achieved independence.

The Bangladesh Liberation War left many Bangladeshi cities in ruins.

The Young Nation

In early 1972, the new Bangladesh had its first prime minister when Mujibur Rahman was released from Pakistani prison. But the new prime minister and the young country faced many difficulties. A flood soon devastated much of the region

Food is distributed to starving flood victims in 1974. Hundreds of thousands of people died from disease and starvation following the floods.

leaving people without homes. Crops were damaged, food was limited, and many hospitals and schools were unusable. That disaster was followed by another: a cholera epidemic. Between the disease and the widespread starvation, many people died.

As he dealt with Bangladesh's troubles, Mujibur Rahman began gathering more power for himself. He banned many newspapers and ended other freedoms. He was assassinated in late 1975.

Soon, Bangladesh came under Zia ur-Rahman's military rule. He allowed greater freedom than Mujibur Rahman had. He worked to improve Bangladesh's infrastructure. He increased food production and supported education. He also supported a political system with many parties, and he won a general election in 1979. But the young country was still unstable, and he was assassinated by army officers in 1981.

Vice president Abdus Sattar temporarily became president but was overthrown by Hussain Muhammad Ershad, the former chief of staff of the Bangladeshi army. He immediately suspended the country's constitution, establishing martial law and putting the military in charge of the country. He wanted to become the country's legitimate president, so he formed his own political party, the National Party, and called for elections. Other parties boycotted the election in October 1986, so Ershad easily won. The opposition parties wanted to force Ershad to step down. They held strikes and protests in support

Zia ur-Rahman was an army general before he became president.

of democracy. In 1988, Bangladesh was once again hit with flooding. When the government did not give the people the help they needed, protests increased to the point that Ershad was forced to resign. He was later convicted of corruption and the illegal possession of weapons.

Recent Times

In recent decades, government action in Bangladesh has been hampered by hostile relations between the nation's two major parties, the Awami League and the Bangladesh Nationalist Party

Awami League supporters shout during a protest in Dhaka.

(BNP). The country has frequently been rocked by anti-government demonstrations, strikes, and allegations of corruption.

In 1991, BNP leader Khaleda Zia, widow of Zia ur-Rahman, became prime minister. Under her rule, a parliamentary form of government was reinstated. She also worked to reform the nation's economy. But change was slow, and her efforts were stalled by a devastating cyclone that hit in 1991. About 139,000 people were killed.

Khaleda Zia was replaced in 1996 by Awami League leader Sheikh Hasina Wazed, the daughter of Mujibur Rahman. Under her rule, the economy continued to slowly improve, as did Bangladesh's relations with India.

After the next election, in 2001, Khaleda Zia again became prime minister. Then in 2009, Sheikh Hasina Wazed became prime minister again. Despite the political unrest that has continued to roil Bangladesh in recent decades, the country has become more stable, and its economy has grown.

Khaleda Zia speaks to supporters during a strike in 1987. Four years later, she became Bangladesh's first female prime minister.

CHAPTER 5

A Long Fight

I N THE BATTLE TO GAIN INDEPENDENCE, THE PEOPLE OF Bangladesh have fought hard. Many have risked their lives and some have lost their lives. Bangladeshis have sometimes chosen trustworthy, reliable leaders, but other times corrupt people have gained power. As a result, Bangladesh is mired in an ongoing search for a stable government.

Opposite: **A member of Bangladesh's presidential guard. The presidential guard is responsible for ensuring the safety of the president and heads of state visiting from other countries.**

The Structure of Government

Like most governments throughout the world, the government of Bangladesh has three branches: executive, judicial, and legislative.

The executive branch is made up of the president, who is elected by the national parliament, and the prime minister, who is appointed by the president. The president's term is limited to five years. The prime minister has no term limits. Under

The National Flag

Bangladesh's flag is simple—a red circle on a green background—but filled with meaning. The green field represents the rich, fertile soil that is needed for farming. The red circle in the middle stands for both the rising sun and the sacrifice the people have made to gain their country's independence. The flag was adopted on January 17, 1972.

The red circle on Bangladesh's flag is offset so it looks centered when the flag is flying.

Changing the System

Bangladeshi lawyer Sara Hossain has worked tirelessly to improve the lives of women and girls in her country. As part of a group called the Bangladesh Legal Aid and Services Trust, she drafted a law on violence against women. She has also challenged degrading punishments against women accused of crimes.

Hossain studied at the University of Oxford in England before becoming a lawyer. She began practicing in the Supreme Court of Bangladesh. In 2016, she received an International Woman of Courage award from the U.S. government. The award recognizes women who work for justice and human rights around the world.

Sara Hossain is one of the most prominent lawyers in Bangladesh.

Sheikh Hasina Wazed has been a major figure in Bangladeshi politics for decades. She began her third term as prime minister in 2014.

the Bangladeshi constitution, the prime minister has the most power. The president can only act upon the advice of both the prime minister and the cabinet, a group of top advisers.

Bangladesh's legislative branch is made up of a one-house parliament called the Jatiya Sangsad, or House of the People. The parliament has 350 seats. Since 2004, 45 of those seats have been reserved for women. Members of parliament are elected by the people for five-year terms.

The judicial branch consists of the nation's courts. The Supreme Court is Bangladesh's highest court. Its judges are appointed by the president. They serve until the age of sixty-seven, when they must retire. The Supreme Court both reviews decisions made in lower courts and has a High Court division that tries major cases itself. Types of lower courts include district courts and magistrate courts. Magistrate courts handle many minor criminal cases, which do not require a full trial.

Political Parties

There are thirty political parties active in Bangladesh. The largest parties in the country are the Bangladesh Nationalist Party, the Jatiya Party, and the Awami League. The Bangladesh

The Bangladesh parliament building was designed by renowned American architect Louis Kahn.

Welcome to Dhaka

More than ten million people live in the capital city of Dhaka. Getting from one place to another in the bustling city is not easy. Dhaka has been called the rickshaw capital of the world. Rickshaws are three-wheeled bicycles with a passenger seat. More than four hundred thousand of these brightly decorated vehicles vie for position on Dhaka's roads with countless cars, buses, motorbikes, and bicycles. Horns honk. Bells ring. Drivers yell. The traffic flows over to the city's Buriganga River, where boats full of goods and passengers push their way through the muddy water.

Dhaka is a mix of old and new. The oldest part of the city is called Old Dhaka. It is filled with historic buildings from a time when the region was under first Mughal and then British control. These include ancient religious

Ahsan Manzil, once the palace of the ruler in Dhaka, is now the site of the National Museum.

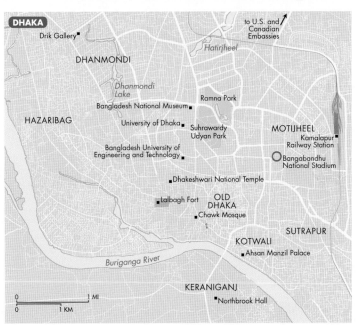

structures such as the Chawk Mosque and the Dhakeshwari National Temple, a Hindu building. Old Dhaka also features nonreligious buildings such as Lalbagh Fort, which dates to the seventeenth century, and Northbrook Hall, which was built during the British period.

In Old Dhaka and around the city, there are many old markets where street food, fruit, and handmade souvenirs are sold. The city also has many modern shopping malls. Dhaka is the site of the Ahsan Manzil Palace, which dates back to the fifteenth century, as well as the Jamuna Future Park, which features more than five hundred stores, an indoor swimming pool, a roller coaster, and a children's theme park.

Today, Dhaka is an important industrial city, with many people working in factories that produce clothing, ceramics, electronics, chemicals, and much more. The city is also an educational center for the country. It is home to many universities, including the University of Dhaka and the Bangladesh University of Engineering and Technology.

Bangladesh's National Government

Executive Branch

President

Prime Minister

Legislative Branch

Parliament
(350 members)

Judicial Branch

Supreme Court

District Courts

Magistrate Courts

Nationalist Party tends to be socially conservative and is often supported by people who want Islam to have a stronger role in society. The Jatiya Party is also conservative. The Awami League is more liberal and nonreligious. It holds by far the most seats in parliament. A Bangladeshi has to be eighteen years old in order to vote.

Military

As soon as Bangladesh became independent, it established a military. The country has an army, navy, and air force, with approximately 137,000 armed forces altogether. All members of the Bangladeshi military are volunteers. People must be at least seventeen years old to serve.

National Anthem

Bangladesh's national anthem, "Amar Shonar Bangla" ("My Golden Bengal"), was written in 1905 by Rabindranath Tagore, a Bengali writer who was born in Calcutta, India, and later moved to what is now Bangladesh. Tagore is the only person to have written two poems used as national anthems: one for Bangladesh and one for India ("Jana Gana Mana"). The music to Bangladesh's national anthem was written by Gagan Harkara. Bangladesh adopted the anthem in 1971.

English translation

My Bengal of Gold, I love you.
Forever your skies,
Your air set my heart in tune
As if it were a flute.
In Spring, O mother mine,
The fragrance from your mango groves,
Makes me wild with joy.
Ah, what a thrill!
In autumn, O mother mine,
In the full blossomed paddy fields
I have seen spread all over the sweet
    smiles.
Ah, what beauty, what shades,

What an affection, and what tenderness!
What a quilt have you spread
At the feet of banyan trees
And along the banks of rivers!
Oh mother mine, words from your lips are
    like
Nectar to my ears!
Ah, what a thrill!
But black parents face when khani
I was struck.
My eyes filled with tears and
Special Bengali,
I love you.

CHAPTER 6

Looking Up

FOR YEARS, BANGLADESH HAS BEEN ONE OF THE POOR-est countries in the world. Too many people and too little land there often meant not enough food and not enough jobs for Bangladeshis. Fortunately, the economic situation in the country has been looking up.

A decade ago, about 45 percent of Bangladeshis were living below the poverty level. Today, that number is closer to 30 percent. The country's gross domestic product (GDP), the total value of goods and services produced in the country, is also growing quickly.

Economic Development

Many factors have contributed to Bangladesh's economic development. One is the large number of nongovernmental organizations (NGOs) active in Bangladesh. NGOs are

Opposite: **A farmer picks guavas to take to a floating market in southern Bangladesh. Hundreds of boats laden with guavas gather at these markets.**

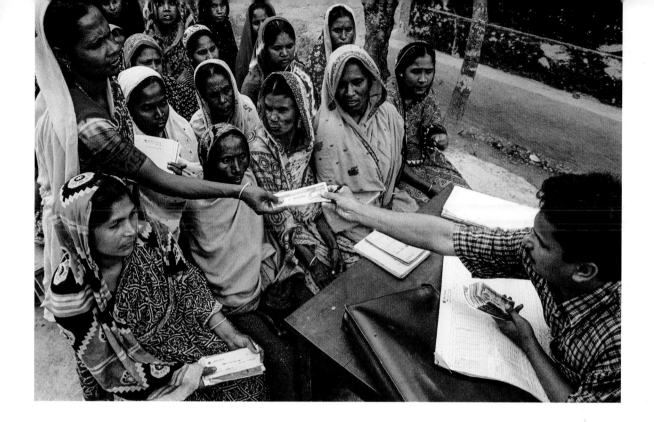

Bangladeshi women take out microloans to help run their small businesses.

independent organizations that work in fields such as education, health care, public policy, and human rights. Bangladesh is the site of the Bangladesh Rural Advancement Committee (BRAC), the world's largest NGO. It has created thousands of small primary schools, improved health care, and provided disaster relief.

One of BRAC's largest and oldest initiatives is a system for giving out microloans. Microloans are very small loans that are given to poor people in need, usually women. The small loans can be used for many purposes. Farmers can use them to buy livestock, for example, or craftspeople can buy necessary supplies. Microloans are a highly effective way of helping people improve their standard of living. About 98 percent of BRAC's microloans are repaid.

Money Facts

The currency used in Bangladesh is called the taka. One taka is divided into one hundred poisha. Coins come in values of 50 poisha and 1, 2, and 5 taka. Bills are printed in values of 2, 5, 10, 20, 50, 100, 500, and 1,000 taka. All bills have an image of Sheikh Mujibur Rahman on the front. On most bills, the reverse depicts an important building. For example, the 100-taka bill features the Star Mosque in Dhaka on the back. In 2018, $1 was equal to 83 taka.

Each denomination of Bangladeshi currency has a different dominant color.

Bangladeshi economist Muhammad Yunus pioneered the idea of microloans, which are now used throughout the world. In 2006, he won the Nobel Peace Prize for his work.

Muhammad Yunus (front, center) founded the Grameen ("rural" in Bengali) Bank to give microloans.

From Field to Factory

Jute is a useful fiber that is often made into rope or twine. About 85 percent of all the world's jute is grown in the Ganges Delta of Bangladesh and India.

It takes a long time to process jute leaves and turn them into a finished product. The shoots can grow as long as 15 feet (5 m) but are only the width of a finger. Workers gather these tall shoots in bundles and tie them together. Next, the shoots are left to dry until their leaves fall off. Now comes the time-consuming part. The stalks are soaked for an entire month so that they soften.

After this, the fiber is stripped from the plants and washed. The strips of fiber are then draped over poles to dry in the sun.

The jute strips are then bundled up again, loaded on boats, and sent to mills. At the mills, the fiber is spun into a tough, resilient twine that can be used to make many products.

After jute is dried, bundles of it are brought to markets where they are sold for processing at factories.

In the Fields

Just under half of all Bangladeshis work in agriculture. Most of them farm rice. It is eaten in Bangladesh and is also one of the nation's top exports. A number of farmers grow and harvest rice with traditional techniques, using sticks to dig holes for seeds and cattle to pull a plow through the fields. In the past, some farmers have struggled to keep their rice fields irrigated, especially when growing boro rice, a type that requires much higher levels of watering. To help solve this problem, scientists from the Bangladesh Agricultural University came up

There are more than twenty-five million cattle in Bangladesh, many of them used to plow fields.

with a new farming method for boro rice. It needs only half as much water as traditional methods. So far, this new technique is working well and scientists are traveling around Bangladesh to teach farmers how to use it.

Another agricultural product common in Bangladesh is jute. Jute is a fiber made from plant stems. It is used to make twine and rope, which are then used in baskets, matting, fishing nets, and the tough backing on carpets.

Workers spread chili peppers out to dry at a factory in Bangladesh.

What Bangladesh Grows, Makes, and Mines

Agriculture (2017)

Rice	32,650,000 metric tons
Jute	2,000,000 metric tons
Wheat	1,115,000 metric tons

Manufacturing

Textiles (2016)	$31.8 billion in exports
Cement (2017)	32 million metric tons
Shoes and hats (2016)	$578 million in exports

Mining

Natural Gas (2015)	14.16 trillion cubic feet
Coal (2013)	845,000 metric tons

Time for Tea

Tea plantations are found in many parts of Bangladesh, but especially in the Sylhet Hills in the northeast. Between March and December, more than one hundred thousand people harvest tea. In the small town of Srimangal, about 100 miles (160 km) outside of Dhaka, there are about 150 tea plantations, earning the town the title "the tea capital of Bangladesh."

A lot of work goes into growing and harvesting tea. During the eight-month plucking season, workers—primarily women—stand in the middle of tall, green, leafy fields, often up to their waists, and pluck the small buds and young leaves from the tea bushes. The workers stay in the fields from sunrise

Women pick tea on a farm in the Sylhet Hills. To get the best flavor, workers must pick two leaves and a bud when harvesting tea.

to sundown, seven days a week. They carry big bags on their shoulders and fill them up with the buds, which are measured and then loaded onto trucks for a trip to the factories. There, the leaves are dried and exported throughout the world.

In addition to tea, Bangladesh grows wheat in the southern part of the country, along with sugarcane, potatoes, tobacco, spices, and fruit. While some portion of these products is exported, much of them goes toward feeding people in Bangladesh.

Fishing

Bangladesh has many rivers and wetlands as well as a long ocean shoreline, so fishing is common in the country. Fishers, known as *majhi*, go out every morning and spend hours on the water hoping to fill their handheld nets with enough fish to both feed their families and sell extra at the market. Unfortunately, because of overfishing, pollution, and environmental damage, the overall number of fish available to be caught is shrinking. Fewer fish to catch means fewer to eat. Between 1991 and 2010, Bangladesh's consumption of fish declined by a third.

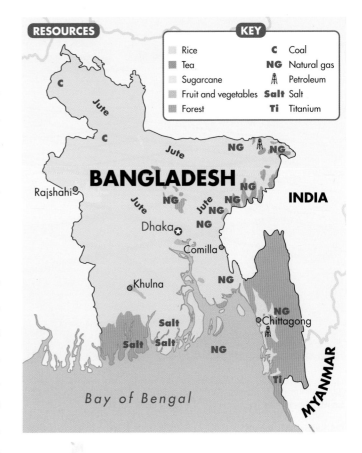

The drop in the number of fish is global. Because of this decline, many parts of the world are turning to aquaculture, or fish farming. In 2017, fish farms, where fish or shellfish are born, raised, and harvested, accounted for half of all the fish consumed across the planet. Bangladeshis began investing in aquaculture in the 1980s, and the result has been successful. In fact, the country is the world's sixth-largest producer of farmed fish and shellfish.

While this has meant more fish for the people to eat, recent studies have shown that the fish from a fish farm do not provide the same nutrition as fish captured naturally. When the majhi catch fish from their boats, they typically capture fish of a number of different species. The fish tend to be small, so the whole fish is eaten—fish, meat, bones, and head. This adds many minerals and vitamins to the diet of those who consume them. The fish from farms, however, are a limited number of species and are grown fairly large. Only the meat is consumed, leaving out many of the nutrients gained by eating the entire smaller fish. For many Bangladeshis, these nutrients are important.

Some farmers in Bangladesh have converted their fields into shrimp and prawn farms. Frozen seafood is the nation's third-largest export, after clothing and jute.

Livestock

About half of the people in Bangladesh own livestock. Some cattle are used to plow fields while others provide food. The hides of some cattle are used to make leather goods, one of the country's biggest exports. Other livestock raised in Bangladesh include buffalo, poultry, goats, and sheep.

Manufacturing

Nearly 30 percent of Bangladeshis work in industry. One of the nation's largest industries is clothing production for top brands and retailers in Europe and North America. The country has more than five thousand garment factories, which employ more than 1.5 million people. Most of these employees are young women between the ages of fourteen and twenty-nine. They work long hours, often between fourteen and sixteen hours a day.

The garment industry has grown tremendously in Bangladesh in recent years. It is now second only to China in the amount of clothing it produces.

Made by Hand

Some of the crafts made in Bangladesh today have a long history in the country. Like Bangladeshis in the past, people today make decorated terra-cotta pots covered in intricate designs and bright colors. These pots are used to store food or carry liquids, but they are also shipped throughout the world for use as decoration.

Weaving straw and bamboo mats is common throughout Bangladesh. In addition to selling their products in the market,

Workers sew clothes at a garment factory in Dhaka. Clothing accounts for more than half of all Bangladesh's exports.

Dangerous Factories

In 2013, an eight-story garment industry building called the Rana Plaza collapsed, killing more than 1,100 people and injuring 2,500 more. The reasons behind the collapse were clear: The building was constructed of substandard materials. It had too many floors with too much heavy equipment on them, and it had received lax inspections. The generators in the factory caused the entire building to shake. Workers were understandably worried, but the Rana family, who owned the business, reassured them they were safe.

Out of this tragedy came improvements. Companies, trade unions, and workers' rights groups banded together to make Bangladeshi buildings safer. These changes included adding sprinkler systems and emergency exits. An agreement called the Accord on Fire and Building Safety was signed between global retailers and trade unions stating that they would only do business with those Bangladeshi factories that pass inspections and follow all safety codes.

Bangladeshis use the mats to pray, sit, and sleep on, as well as cover their floors. The mats incorporate many different types of leaves and colored straw to create complex patterns and designs.

Leather finishing is a long-standing craft in Bangladesh, and it has become one of the nation's top industries. Bangladesh has a reputation worldwide for products made from buffalo, cow, sheep, and goat hides. The country has hundreds of tanneries, plus dozens of manufacturing plants specializing in footwear. More than a half a million people work in these factories.

While the leather-finishing industry provides many jobs, it also puts workers at risk. A lot of leatherwork uses toxic chemicals. These chemicals can sicken the workers, who are sometimes as young as eleven years old. Virtually none of the employees are provided with safety equipment or even basic gloves and footwear. The tanneries are also an environmental hazard because much of their waste product is released directly into local waterways.

A craftsperson weaves fibers from the murta plant to make a mat. Murta is famed for feeling cool to the skin.

Recalling an Ancient Tradition

Some ancient Bangladeshi crafts are being lost. For thousands of years, wooden boats and barges traveled along Bangladesh's many waterways. Today, most of those wooden boats are gone. They have been replaced by speedy powerboats. A preservationist named Runa Khan is trying to change that.

In 1994, Khan learned how to restore wooden boats and fell in love with the process. Knowing how important wooden boatbuilding was to her country's history, she has been working to preserve the tradition so it could be shared with other young people. "The beautiful, ancient boats were disappearing," Khan says, "and the old-world carpentry skills were dying before your eyes. We had to fight to preserve what was becoming only a memory."

Khan assembled a team of talented craftspeople, including carpenters, sail makers, rope makers, and blacksmiths, who began creating model boats. Khan's team has created more than 150 replica ships and she intends to open a boat museum, so that young people can appreciate this vital part of Bangladeshi history.

A worker in Chittagong builds a traditional wooden fishing boat.

"It will be a place where people can experience the reality of boats and watch carpenters as they work—a living museum with boats floating on the river."

Because of the environmental impact of leather factories, the High Court ruled that these industries needed to be moved out of Dhaka to an industrial park. It has been a slow process and does not solve the fundamental problems associated with the industry.

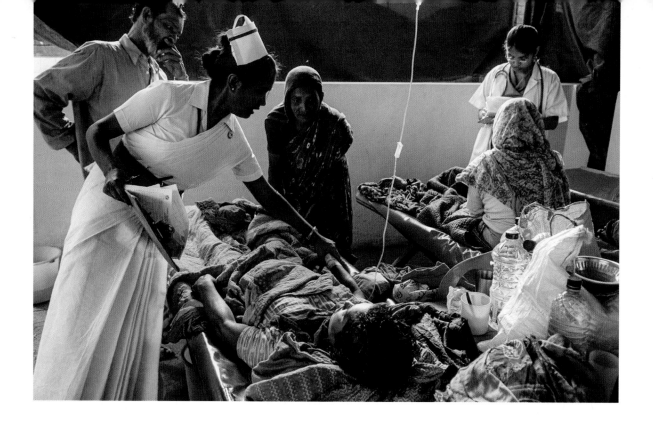

Resources

Bangladesh has a large supply of natural gas, which provides much of the country's electricity. Coal is also found underground in Bangladesh. Some coal mines are active in the northwestern part of the country.

Services

Services make up the largest part of the Bangladeshi economy. Service industries include fields such as banking, education, health care, tourism, and sales. Bangladesh has a large banking industry. It also welcomes a growing number of tourists. People come from all over the world to visit the beaches at Cox's Bazar, paddle a boat through the mangroves, and explore ancient palaces.

Nurses tend to patients at a hospital in Bangladesh. About a third of Bangladeshis work in service industries.

CHAPTER 7

Being a Bangladeshi

THE PEOPLE OF BANGLADESH HAVE HAD TO COPE with many problems, from floods to poverty, and many have done so through determination, faith, and an ongoing hope that life will get better. Food and water may be limited, but it is shared.

In rural areas, homes are made out of whatever material is plentiful. This includes mud, bamboo, and wood. Many rural houses are built on stilts to help protect the homes from floodwaters. Few homes have electricity or plumbing.

In the City

While many Bangladeshis live in rural villages, an increasing number have moved into the nation's largest cities in search of better opportunities.

Finding room for everyone to live in Bangladesh can

Opposite: **Rickshaws fill a street in Dhaka. They are the most common form of transportation in many Bangladeshi cities.**

Mud homes have many advantages. The thick walls keep the interior cool, and there is no danger of the houses burning.

A House Made of Mud

Some houses found in Bangladesh are made out of mud. Large cities rarely include these homes. Most are found in rural areas and around small cities, especially those in the drier regions, where floods rarely reach. These mud houses have been built in Bangladesh for hundreds of years.

The majority of them are rectangular and stand 20 to 30 feet (6 to 9 m) tall. The walls tend to be between 1.5 and 3 feet (0.5 and 1 m) thick. Windows are simply areas left open during construction. Bamboo is used for supporting beams and columns. Thatch (dried grass), *golpata* (mangrove leaves), and tile are commonly used for the roof. While these homes are comfortable, they are at special risk of cracking or collapsing from floods, earthquakes, or high winds.

be difficult. The cities are over-crowded. In many cities, there are not enough apartment buildings and houses to accommodate everyone. In and near these cities, shantytowns, or bustees, have grown up. Families crowd into rows of closely packed thatched houses. Young children run up and down the dirt paths between them, and sometimes line up in front of water pumps to get water for their family.

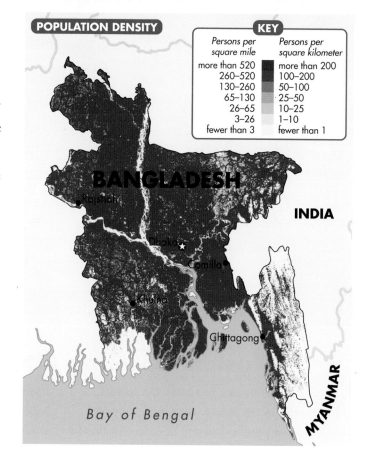

Changing Families

Traditionally, Bangladeshi families were large, with at least four children. That has been changing in recent years. Government organizations and international groups have worked together to encourage family planning, and families have gotten smaller. Today, most Bangladeshi families have two children.

In Bangladesh, extended families are close. Children, parents, and grandparents typically share the same home. Married sons and their families often continue living at home. It is their job to take care of their elders when it becomes necessary.

The country is male-dominated. In most families, the eldest male is responsible for making major decisions. Women are in charge of cooking, taking care of the children, and looking after animals and livestock.

Population of Major Cities (2018 est.)

Dhaka	10,356,500
Chittagong	3,920,222
Khulna	1,342,339
Rajshahi	700,133
Comilla	389,411

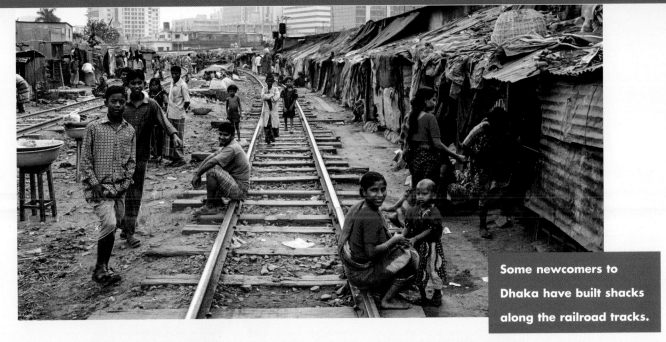

Fastest Growing City in the World

In recent years, Dhaka has been the fastest growing city in the world. Each year, almost half a million people move to Dhaka. The United Nations has predicted that by 2025, the city's population will top twenty million. That would make it larger than Mexico City, Mexico, or Beijing or Shanghai, China.

Although Dhaka is growing quickly, it is a relatively poor city, without the infrastructure and resources to support the newcomers. As much as half the city is made up of shantytowns, often enveloped in a blue smoky haze from open fires used for cooking. Overcrowding, lack of sufficient water and food, and energy shortages make life in Dhaka difficult. Because of these problems, it is sometimes called the "megacity of the poor."

In 2017, a number of housing projects were approved in Dhaka. More than 130 buildings, containing more than fifteen thousand individual apartments, will be built for middle- and low-income families. Although these apartments will accommodate just a small percentage of the people who need housing, it is a start.

This picture is changing, however. The country now has a female prime minister, and the number of seats held by women in Bangladesh's parliament increases every year. In addition, more women are working outside of the home. Most of them are employed in the garment industry, but many also work in industries that produce frozen foods, handicrafts, and leather goods.

A decade ago, most Bangladeshis did not live past age sixty. This, too, has been improving. In 2017, the life expectancy for men in Bangladesh was seventy-one and for women it was seventy-six.

Education

In years past, many Bangladeshi children were not able to go to school. Some children were needed at home to work. In other cases, families couldn't afford the expense of school. This has

Children at a school in the Chittagong Hills. About four out of five Bangladeshi children complete primary school.

Salman Khan at work in California. Khan Academy videos on YouTube have been viewed 1.5 billion times.

Online Education

Educator and entrepreneur Salman Amin Khan was born in Louisiana to a Bangladeshi father and Indian mother. After graduating from the Massachusetts Institute of Technology with a master's degree in business administration, he began working as a financial analyst.

In 2006, Khan began tutoring his cousin in math via YouTube videos. His videos gained a great deal of attention, and they soon had millions of viewers. In 2009, he quit his job and focused on making online videos full time. Today, the Khan Academy is used by students all over the world as a virtual way to enhance their education.

changed dramatically. In 2015, 98 percent of young children were enrolled in primary school (grades 1 through 5). About 54 percent go on to attend secondary school (grades 6 to 10).

The country's literacy rate reflects this change in school attendance. A decade ago, 43 percent of adults in Bangladesh could read and write. By 2017, about 73 percent were literate.

While more Bangladeshis are going to school, the quality

of their education varies tremendously. National learning assessments have shown that many students have weak reading skills, and few have mastered basic math skills.

Bangladesh has thirty-nine public universities, including the University of Dhaka, Chittagong Medical University, the Bangladesh University of Engineering and Technology, and the University of Rajshahi. The University of Dhaka is the nation's oldest, established in 1921. It is also the largest, serving about thirty-three thousand students.

Language

The fact that the Bengalis once went to the battlefield in order to fight for their own language emphasizes how important language is to them. It is a source of cultural identity and pride. When Pakistani officials tried to force them to accept Urdu as the national language, people objected—and some

Bengali Words and Phrases

Hae/Jee	**Yes**
Na/Jee na	**No**
Dhonno-baad	**Thank You**
Nomoshkar	**Hello/Good-bye**
Kemon achhen?	**How are you?**
Bhaalo ache.	**I am fine.**
Apnar naam kee?	**What is your name?**
Amar naam . . .	**My name is . . .**
Buj-tey paarchhi na	**I don't understand.**
Maaf ko-roon/Khoma ko-roon	**Sorry**

The Bengali writing system includes a line on top of the letters.

even gave up their lives in the fight. In the end, Bengali (also referred to as Bangla) was made an official language.

Bengali is related to the ancient Sanskrit language. It also includes words that come from other languages, including Persian, Portuguese, Arabic, and Hindi.

The writing system used for Bengali is ornate, and it does not use capital letters.

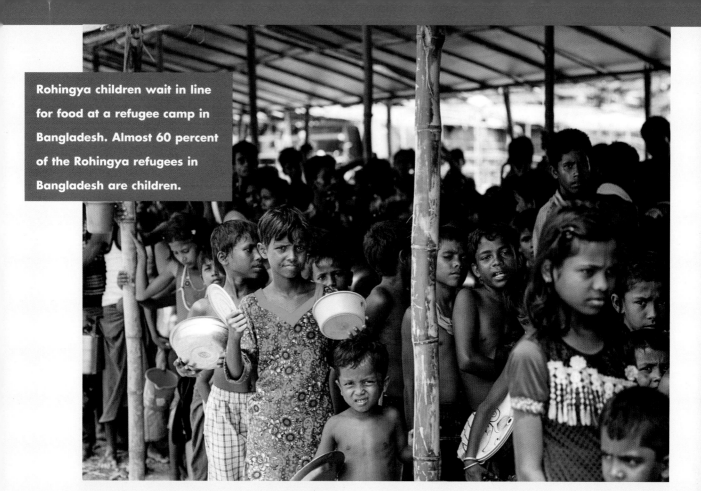

Rohingya children wait in line for food at a refugee camp in Bangladesh. Almost 60 percent of the Rohingya refugees in Bangladesh are children.

The Rohingya Refugee Crisis

Bangladesh is a crowded country. But recent events in the neighboring nation of Myanmar have brought even more people in.

The Rohingya are a Muslim minority group in Myanmar, a predominantly Buddhist nation. Over the years, the Rohingya have sometimes been persecuted in Myanmar, and some refugees fled into Bangladesh as early as the 1970s. But recently, the situation grew much worse. In Myanmar, the Rohingya are denied citizenship and are frequently attacked. Many have no choice but to flee.

Hundreds of thousands of Rohingya have moved into Bangladesh. There, they have gathered in makeshift refugee camps. The buildings are made of bamboo and have no electricity. These camps are overcrowded, and food and water are in short supply. Diseases such as cholera and malaria are thriving in the camps.

The Bangladeshi government has limited resources. The refugee crisis adds a burden on an already struggling nation, so Bangladesh needs outside help to deal with the crisis.

A Different Way of Life

A Chakma woman carries goods to sell at the local market.

The vast majority of people in Bangladesh belong to the Bengali ethnic group. Bengalis are descended from the many different groups of people who migrated into the region over time.

About 2 percent of the population of Bangladesh are not Bengali. They belong to more than thirty ethnic groups. Most of them live in the Chittagong Hills of the southeast.

These minority groups lead a very different lifestyle than the Bengalis. Each group has its own language, customs, and clothing. Most follow Buddhism, although some are Hindu. The largest of these groups is the Chakmas. Approximately three hundred thousand Chakmas live in the Chittagong region of Bangladesh. Another thirty thousand are found in India and Myanmar. The second-largest minority group in Bangladesh is the Marmas. Other groups in the Chittagong Hills include the Tripuras, the Khomois, and the Kukis.

Some minority ethnic groups are also found in other parts of Bangladesh. For example, the Mandis and Hajongs live in the north, while the Manipuris and Khasias are in the northeast. The Santals and Rajbongshis are in the northwest.

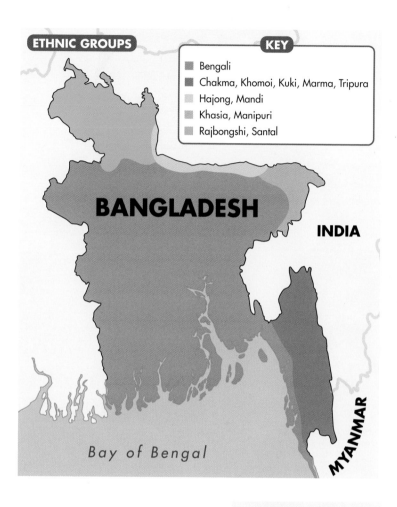

ETHNIC GROUPS

KEY
- ■ Bengali
- ■ Chakma, Khomoi, Kuki, Marma, Tripura
- ■ Hajong, Mandi
- ■ Khasia, Manipuri
- ■ Rajbongshi, Santal

BANGLADESH

INDIA

MYANMAR

Bay of Bengal

Ethnic Groups

Bengali	98%
Biharis, Jummas, and others	2%

CHAPTER 8

Faith and Followers

O VER THE CENTURIES, THE MOST COMMON RELI-gions followed by the people of what is now Bangladesh have shifted. At one time, most people followed the Hindu religion. By the late 1800s, however, Islam had become the primary belief system in Bangladesh. In 1988, it was named the country's official religion and remains so today. By 2013, 89 percent of Bangladeshis were Muslims, people who follow Islam. Other Bangladeshis practice a variety of religions, including Hinduism, Buddhism, Christianity, and animism.

Opposite: **Each year, about two million Muslims gather near Dhaka for the Bishwa Ijtema, or "world congregation." It is the second-largest Muslim gathering in the world after the hajj pilgrimage to Mecca, Saudi Arabia.**

Being Muslim

The religion of Islam arose in the 600s in what is now Saudi Arabia, when a prophet named Muhammad reported that he had received messages from God. Muhammad was said to

have continued receiving messages over many years. These messages were eventually compiled to create the sacred writings of Islam, called the Qur'an.

As part of their religion, Muslims follow the Five Pillars of Islam. These are duties they are expected to follow in their lives. The first is *shahada*, a declaration of faith. This declaration states, "There is no god but God, and Muhammad is the messenger of God."

The second pillar of Islam is *salat*, or prayer. Muslims are supposed to stop their activities and pray five times a day, at dawn, noon, midafternoon, sunset, and night. The call to prayer announcing when it is time to pray is broadcast from minarets, tall towers or mosques. When Muslims pray, they always face in the direction of Mecca, Saudi Arabia. The birthplace of Muhammad, it is the holiest city in Islam.

Major Religions	
Islam	89%
Hinduism	10%
Buddhism	0.6%
Christianity	0.3%
Other	0.1%

Zakat, or charity, is the third pillar of Islam. Muslims have a duty to help those who are in need. Many people make zakat payments during Ramadan.

Sawm, the fourth pillar, requires Muslims to fast, or abstain from eating or drinking, from sunrise to sunset during Ramadan, the ninth month in the Islamic calendar. Fasting during Ramadan is supposed to encourage self-discipline, focus people's attention inward on spiritual matters, and increase people's empathy for the needy. Muslims for whom fasting would be unhealthy, such as pregnant women, the elderly, young children, and the ill, are exempt from the requirement

Baitul Mukarram, the national mosque of Bangladesh, is the largest mosque in the country. It can hold forty thousand people.

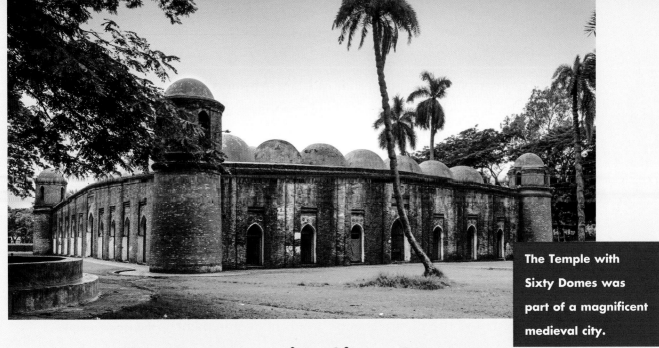

The Temple with Sixty Domes was part of a magnificent medieval city.

The Temple with Sixty Domes

A tour of Shait Gumbad Mosque, or the Temple with Sixty Domes, is something few people forget. Located in the city of Bagerhat, the mosque was built in 1459 by Khan Jahan Ali. Despite its name, the mosque has eighty-one domes, rather than sixty. The temple is made mainly of burnished red bricks. It has massive circular towers at each corner. Inside the mosque are ten rows of six pillars made out of slabs of black stone.

There are ten mihrabs, or niches, inside. One is made of black stone, while the others are made of brick. Over the centuries, the intricate designs on these mihrabs have faded, but tourists can see just enough to realize how beautiful the patterns once were.

The temple's famous domes are found outside. There are seventy-seven on the roof, and four in the massive towers. Each one of them is decorated.

to fast during Ramadan. The fast is broken each evening with a large meal known as *iftar*.

The last pillar of Islam is *hajj*, or pilgrimage. At least once during their lives Muslims are supposed to make a pilgrimage to Mecca if they are physically and financially able.

Major Muslim Holy Days

Islamic New Year

This holiday is typically celebrated quietly, often by reading religious texts at home.

Eid e-Milad-un-Nabi

This day celebrates Muhammad's birthday.

Ramadan

Ramadan is the holiest month of year in the Muslim calendar. During Ramadan, Muslims fast from sunrise to sundown.

Eid al-Fitr

This holy day celebrates the end of Ramadan.

Eid al-Adha

Known as the Feast of Sacrifice, this day honors the prophet Abraham's willingness to sacrifice his son out of obedience to God. It typically involves the slaughter of a lamb that is then cooked and shared with others in honor of Abraham's sacrifice.

Major Hindu Holy Days

Saraswati Puja

This spring festival honors the goddess of knowledge. To celebrate this day, clay statues of the goddess Saraswati are made.

Janmashtami

This holiday celebrates the birthday of the god Krishna.

Holi

To celebrate the end of winter, people go into the streets and smear each other with colored powder and drench each other with water. Holi is sometimes called the Festival of Colors.

Durga Puja

For four days, people honor the mighty warrior goddess, Durga.

Diwali

Diwali, known as the Festival of Lights, celebrates the victory of good over evil. During the five-day festival, lamps are lit as a symbol of hope for the future.

Hindu Beliefs

Roughly 10 percent of Bangladeshis are Hindus. Most live in the western part of the country, in cities such as Khulna, Jessore, Dinajpur, Faridpur, and Barisal.

Hindus believe in a single god, but that one god has many

On a holiday called Holi, Hindus go into the streets and spread colored powders on themselves and each other to celebrate the beginning of spring.

different manifestations, or forms. Hindus sometimes have shrines at home dedicated to a particular manifestation of god. Hindus believe in reincarnation, the idea that the soul does not die but rather returns in different forms. They also believe that the way people behave in this lifetime will be reflected in the next lifetime, a concept known as karma.

In Search of Enlightenment

Less than 1 percent of the people in Bangladesh identify as Buddhists. Most are among the ethnic minority groups that live in the Chittagong Hills. Buddhist beliefs are based on the thought of an Indian prince named Siddhartha Gautama. For six years, he traveled in search of wisdom. He meditated often until he believed he discovered the cause of human suffering and how to achieve enlightenment, an end of that suffering. He decided to spend the rest of his life teaching what he had learned. This is known as the Four Noble Truths: all lives contain suffering, suffering comes from the desire for material items, erasing the desire erases the suffering, and erasing the desire comes from following the path of enlightenment. If people did all of these things, he explained, they would reach nirvana, the state of enlightenment.

People belonging to the Marma ethnic group dance during a Buddhist festival in the Chittagong Hills.

CHAPTER 9

A Chance to Relax

STORYTELLING AND STAGE PERFORMANCES HAVE LONG traditions in Bangladesh. People watch *jatras*, or folk dramas, acted out on stage. To honor those traditions, Dhaka hosts the International Folk Festival. In the years since the festival began in 2014, it has featured many performers from Bangladesh, as well as from Iran, Mali, and India. "Music runs in the blood of Bangladeshi people," says festival sponsor Anjan Chowdhury. "They sing when they go fishing, farming, doing their daily chores." During the festival, all kinds of music is performed, from folk to rock and roll to piano. The music explores Bangladeshi identity and spirituality.

Opposite: **A Bangladeshi woman performs a classical dance form called manipuri. In manipuri, the swaying movements often relate stories from the life of the god Krishna.**

Visual Arts

The role of art in Bangladesh culture has grown in recent decades. The number of art galleries has increased, and events

The National Museum

The Bangladesh National Museum is one of the largest museums in South Asia. It started as a single room a century ago. Today, it fills a four-story building. Located in Dhaka, the museum offers visitors the chance to see the country's history from ancient times to the present. It features one of the largest collections of armor in South Asia, as well as a huge display of embroidered quilts. It also has displays of fossils, gold coins, stone inscriptions, and clothing. While the museum is known for its ancient items, it also features the works of contemporary artists.

such as the Dhaka Art Summit are attracting ever larger crowds. Dhaka's art galleries exhibit work spanning from the most traditional arts to contemporary graphic art and photography. The Drik Gallery is the largest privately owned gallery in the country. Opened in 1993, it focuses on exhibiting photos. Some of these photos display the beauty of Bangladeshi scenery, while others show dark and dangerous moments such as the Rana Plaza collapse.

Literature

Bengali written literature dates back thousands of years. When Muslims first arrived in the region, they brought with

A visitor photographs works at the Dhaka Art Summit. The exhibition features work by more than three hundred artists.

them a respect and appreciation of literature, and soon a number of Bengali poets were writing verses. One of the best-known writers to emerge from this region was Rabindranath Tagore. The son of a Hindu author and philosopher, Tagore wrote extensively during his lifetime. He penned thousands of poems and songs, as well as two dozen plays, and many novels and short story collections. In 1913, he was awarded the Nobel Prize in Literature for his sensitive poetry. He was the first non-European to win the prize. Tagore is considered a legend throughout Bangladesh.

Bangladesh's national poet is Kazi Nazrul Islam, the "rebel poet." Many of his thousands of songs and poems focus on religious and social oppression and prejudice. His work was so respected that, in 1985, the Nazrul Institute was opened to carry out research on the Bangladesh culture.

A number of Bengali authors have been getting attention worldwide in recent years. Tahmima Anam's *The Good Muslim* was named one of the *New Yorker*

Rabindranath Tagore changed Bengali literature by writing about personal and political themes rather than classical and religious subjects.

magazine's best books of the year. Writer-editor Farah Ghuznavi published a collection of short stories, called *Lifelines*, by fifteen young Bengali women.

K. Anis Ahmed published an anthology titled *Good Night, Mr. Kissinger*. Ahmed wrote about how he remembered Dhaka,

Tahmima Anam's first novel, *A Golden Age*, was based upon her parents' story of being young fighters in the Bangladesh Liberation War.

compared to what it is like there today: "I grew up bicycling freely through the neighborhood, and at times far beyond, in the '80s. Today, it is unimaginable for any 10-year-old to be able to do that in any part of Dhaka. The city is now heavily inflected by near-constant chaos, congestion, confinement, and provocation, including, at times, sudden violence." He went on to say, "I lived for seven years in New York, and compared to the intensity of Dhaka, I found New York idyllic. My stories are about finding a vocabulary for this new urban intensity."

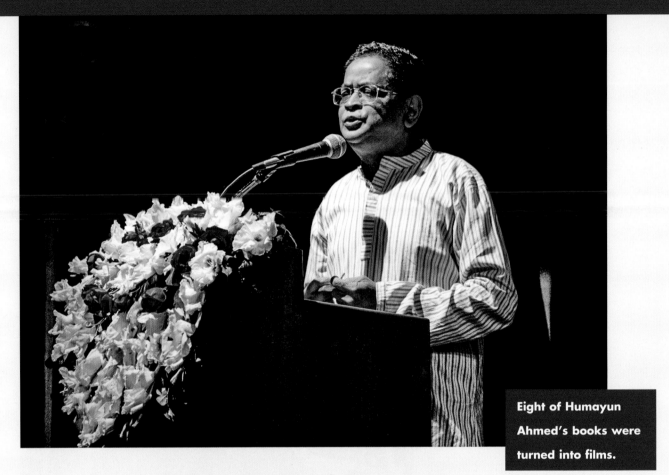

Eight of Humayun Ahmed's books were turned into films.

A Bangladeshi Storyteller

On November 13, 2017, Google featured a new doodle designed to honor what would have been the sixty-ninth birthday of Bangladeshi writer Humayun Ahmed (1948–2012). Ahmed went to school to become a chemist, but ended up trading that career for being an author. Over his lifetime, he wrote more than two hundred books, both fiction and nonfiction. He also wrote a number of television shows. He won multiple awards for his work and was honored across Bangladesh for his contributions to language, film, and literature.

Ahmed's works were often funny and irreverent. They captured the traditions and aspirations of average Bangladeshis. His first novel was published in 1972, and in 1983, his first television show, *Prothom Prohor*, aired. His most popular TV program, *Kothao Keu Nei*, was a drama centered on the exploits of a gangster. In 1994, Ahmed's first film, *Aguner Poroshmoni*, was released.

In the Google doodle, Ahmed is shown in his home of Nuhash Polli, an estate he filled with statues and wildlife from around the world. He is enjoying a pot of tea and reading a book. The drawing shows the author meeting Himu, a well-loved character from some of his novels.

Sports

Soccer is the favorite sport among Bangladeshis. The second most popular sport is cricket, a ball-and-bat game that was brought to the country by the British. Bangladeshis both play the game and show their support for the Tigers, the national cricket team. Less than a quarter of the population owns a television, so people tend to gather in groups when it is time to watch the game.

The official sport of Bangladesh is called *kabaddi*. It was declared the national sport in 1972 by Prime Minister Mujibur Rahman. Historians believe he chose it because it had its roots in Bangladesh rather than Great Britain. Kabaddi is played by two teams, each with twelve players. A "raider" is

A young Bangladeshi man plays cricket in the middle of a rice field.

selected and sent into the opponent's court, yelling "Kabaddi, kabaddi!" Then the raider takes the deepest breath he or she can and begins tagging as many players as possible before taking another breath.

Kabaddi is popular throughout South Asia, and is played in the villages and towns of Bangladesh. It is also played professionally and is part of many international competitions. Between 1990 and 2014, Bangladeshi kabaddi players earned fifteen medals in the Asian Games, the South Asian Games, the Asian Championship, and the World Cup.

People playing kabaddi in Dhaka. The sport is popular throughout South Asia.

Enchantment of the World Bangladesh

Hula-Hooping to Help

What do hula-hooping, Bangladesh, and human rights have to do with one another? If you are Bangladeshi Wasfia Nazreen, the answer is everything. In 2010, Nazreen was working with CARE, an international humanitarian aid group. They work to educate and train abused women and children. When the funding for CARE ran out, Nazreen did not know what to do next. She decided to go in a different direction. An amateur mountain climber, she wanted to find a way to combine activism and climbing.

She started by selling what she had and getting a number of loans. She created the Bangladesh on Seven Summits Foundation and set out to climb the seven highest mountain peaks in the world. This would make her the first Bangladeshi to climb all these peaks.

Each time she reached a peak, she put up a Bangladesh flag. She also hula-hooped using a hoop in Bengali colors. "Eighty percent of the people [in Bangladesh] haven't seen a mountain," she explained to *National Geographic*. "Going to every continent took the Bangladeshi people to every continent. It gave them a lot of pride."

Why the Hula-Hoop, though?

"When I was a little girl, one of my first memories was of this foreign couple visiting my town," she explained. "I'd never seen white people. Their daughter had this Hula-Hoop. I wanted to play with it. I was trying it, and one of the neighborhood women said something along the lines of 'Girls shouldn't be shaking their hips.' The way she said it had this very derogatory meaning. I thought, Good girls can't play with Hula-Hoops.

"This was taken from my life—the right to play as a little girl. I was told I couldn't bike. . . . I'm doing this for myself and for the little girls back at home. It's my little way of saying, 'No more.'"

CHAPTER 10

A Welcoming Land

ASK VISITORS WHAT THEY REMEMBER MOST ABOUT traveling in Bangladesh and the answer most likely will not be the lush tea plantations, the sparkling coastlines, or the crowded cities. Instead, people will remark on the Bangladeshi people themselves. They are considered one of the most hospitable people in the world. Friends and family are always welcome into their homes with enthusiasm, and they typically greet tourists with genuine smiles.

Opposite: **Bangladesh is a young country. About 47 percent of the people are under age twenty-five.**

Clothing

Staying cool in Bangladesh is often challenging. Light, loose clothing helps make the heat more tolerable. What people wear depends, in large part, on their religion. Muslim men, for example, tend to wear a *lungi*, a patterned piece of cloth wrapped around the waist. They pair it with a western-style shirt. Many

Playing Games

Like kids around the world, children in Bangladesh spend lots of time running and playing. They play many different games. They have their own versions of tag, blind man's bluff, and hide-and-seek.

In Bangladesh, hide-and-seek is known as *lukochuri*. Teams of eight to ten people play, with one player being declared the king, and one the thief. The king covers the thief's eyes, while the other players all hide. Then, the thief opens his or her eyes and tries to find each player before they can get to the king. Players touched by the thief become thieves in the next round of the game.

Satchada, or seven tiles, is a team game played with seven flat stones. The stones are stacked on top of each other. One player tries to knock the stack down by throwing a ball at it. Players from the other team scramble to stack the stones back up, while the player throwing the ball aims at them. If the ball touches the players, they are out.

Hindu men wear a *dhoti,* a piece of cloth that wraps around the waist and between the legs like a pair of shorts.

Women tend to wear *saris,* brightly colored pieces of cloth that are up to 18 feet (5.5 m) long. The cloth is wrapped around the waist to form a long skirt, and then brought up over the shoulder to create a partial shirt. A light blouse is worn underneath. Simple white cotton saris are traditionally worn during the week, while silk saris are brought out for special occasions

A worker prints fabric at a market in Dhaka. Many Bangladeshis buy special clothing for Ramadan.

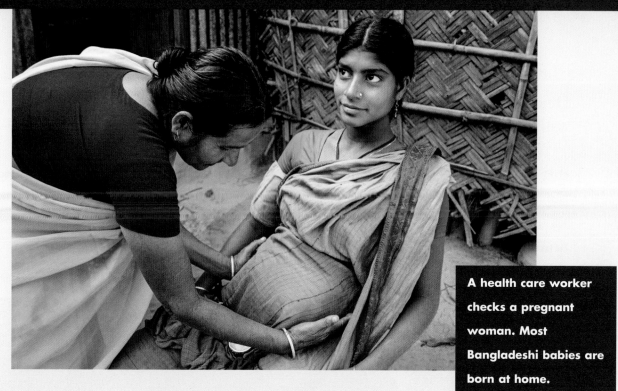

A health care worker checks a pregnant woman. Most Bangladeshi babies are born at home.

Celebrating New Life

During the seventh month of pregnancy, expectant Bengali mothers take part in a *shaad* festival. Similar to American baby showers, these celebrations are designed to nurture the mother-to-be. Female friends and family come over, laden with gifts of the woman's favorite foods.

If the woman has had any cravings, guests try to meet them. The food is not only meant as a gift, but also to ensure that the unborn baby is well nourished. During the celebration, women share childbirth stories and parenting advice, and pray for the health of mother and child.

like weddings and festivals. Some women wear *shalwar kameez*, or loose pants and long tunic tops with a *dupatta*, a shawl or scarf. If the weather requires it, women add shawls over their heads.

From Here to There

There are few cars in Bangladesh. In 2017, fewer than nineteen thousand cars were registered in the whole country.

Instead, Bangladeshis rely on other modes of transportation such as rickshaws and motorcycles. These can get through a city more quickly because they can wind in and around traffic jams. In 2016, the country had more than 11,000 rickshaws registered. However, many owners do not register their rickshaws, so experts believe the number is closer to 180,000. In addition, more than three hundred thousand motorcycles roar through the streets.

Motorcycles are more common than cars in Bangladesh.

Bangladeshi trains are sometimes so crowded that people must ride on top of them.

Given how many waterways crisscross Bangladesh, it makes sense that many people depend on boats to get from one place to another. This is especially true during the rainy season when many roads and bridges are underwater. Rivers are filled with boats of all kinds. There are canoes and "country boats," which are propelled through the water with paddles or long wooden poles. Steamers are used for longer journeys and heavier loads. Ferryboats carry hundreds of people from one shore to another.

Lax safety regulations have turned some of these trips into disasters. Numerous ferries have sunk, some because of faulty equipment, and others because of bad weather. Many accidents are caused because the boats are carrying loads that are too heavy. In May 2014, a ferry bound for Dhaka capsized. Built to handle 100 passengers, it was carrying 250 people. A few passengers were able to jump overboard and swim to shore, but more than a hundred died. Between 2001 and 2014, at least five thousand people lost their lives in ferry accidents.

At the Table

A typical Bangladesh kitchen looks very different from an American kitchen. The stove is usually built into the mud floor. When it is time to eat, families typically sit on the floor around a low table. There are no chairs.

Bangladeshis do not use silverware to eat their food. Instead, they pick the food up with the fingers of their right hand.

The Bangladesh Energy Drink

This light, nutty drink is high in protein and a great start to the day. It's also good with a meal. Have an adult help you with this recipe.

Ingredients

- 2 to 3 tablespoons basil seeds
- 1 cup milk
- Sugar to taste
- 1 teaspoon ground cardamom
- ½ cup shelled pistachios
- ½ cup slivered almonds
- Ice cubes

Directions

1. Start by putting the basil seeds in a bowl of water for ten minutes to soak.
2. Put the milk, sugar, cardamom, pistachios, and almonds in a blender and combine until liquefied.
3. Drain the water from the basil seeds and add the seeds to the mixture. Add 2 to 3 ice cubes and blend again.
4. Pour into a glass and drink!

Traditionally, women have done all the cooking in Bangladesh. Although other gender roles are changing in the country, cooking is still the domain of women.

Rice is the staple food in the Bangladeshi dict. It is boiled or fried, served plain, with vegetables, and with fish and meat, immersed in different flavorful spices, or added to special desserts. Because of the nation's climate, Bangladeshi farmers can grow vegetables year-round. Dishes often include cauliflower, cabbage, potato, peas, carrots, radishes, eggplants, and pumpkins.

Rice is served at every meal in Bangladesh, for breakfast, lunch, and dinner.

Tea appears on the table as often as rice does. Sometimes it is served with milk or sugar, other times with nothing added.

One of the favorite drinks in Bangladesh is *lassi*, a protein-rich drink made from yogurt. Other drinks include sugarcane juice, lime and date juice, and green coconut water.

Mealtime

Breakfast is often served around 8:00 a.m., following morning prayers. It typically consists of boiled rice soaked all night in

water and mixed with salt and green chilies. Other choices include *muri* (puffed rice), *chira* (flattened rice), or *khoi* (popped rice). The rice is usually accompanied by some type of fruit or yogurt.

Lunch tends to be the biggest meal of the day in Bangladesh. In many homes, it is served in the midafternoon, about 2:00 p.m. Popular dishes include rice with fried vegetables, fish, and spices. A traditional Bangladeshi lentil dish called *daal* is also served. This thick soup is full of spices such as turmeric, coriander, cumin, fennel seed, and ginger.

Dinner is served as late as 10:00 p.m. in some parts of the country. It is typically a light meal, made up of rice and vegetables or fruit. The only restaurants in Bangladesh are found in large cities. Otherwise, people tend to either eat at home or grab a quick snack from local markets or street vendors.

Chaat is a popular snack in Bangladesh. It is made of spiced chickpeas, pieces of potato, or bread, and is sometimes served with toppings.

During the month of Ramadan, Muslims fast during the daylight hours. After dark, the fast is broken with a meal called iftar. In some places, iftar is a large communal meal.

National Holidays

Language Movement Day	February 21
Sheikh Mujibur Rahman's birthday	March 17
Independence Day	March 26
Bengali New Year	April 14
May Day	May 1
National Mourning Day	August 15
Janmashtami	August or September
Victory Day	December 16
Christmas	December 25

Several Muslim holidays are also national holidays. But since the Islamic calendar is eleven days shorter than the Western calendar, these dates fall on different days in the Western calendar each year.

Shab e-Barat	Eid al-Adha
Jumatul Bidah	Ashura
Night of Destiny	Eid e-Milad-un Nabi
Eid al-Fitr	

Celebrating Together

Many of the most important holidays in Bangladesh are religious in nature. Some are celebrated by Muslims, and others by Hindus. One of the biggest holidays celebrated by all Bangladeshis is Pahela Baishakh, or Bengali New Year. Each April 14, people celebrate the new year by wearing their most colorful clothes. They attend fairs and festivals. They eat delicious snacks and watch jatra plays. Together, they celebrate being Bengali.

In Dhaka, Bengali New Year is celebrated with a huge procession that features large models and masks of people and animals.

A Welcoming Land

Timeline

Bangladeshi History

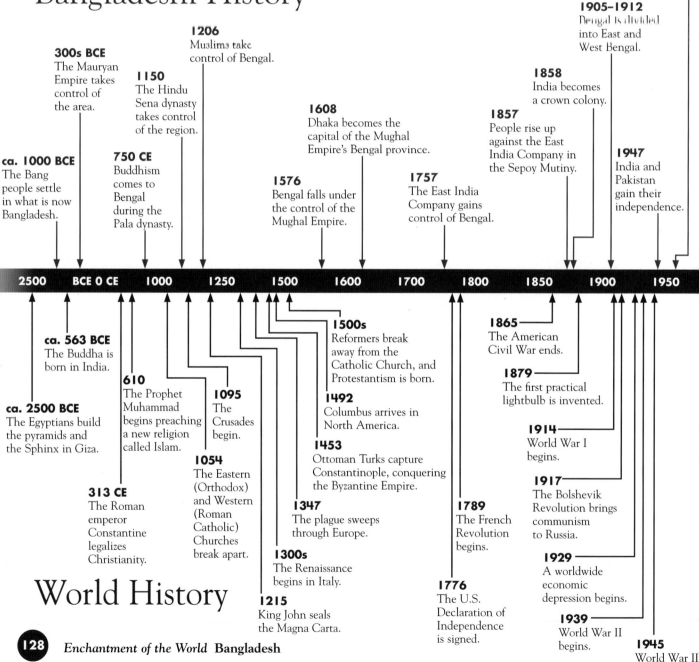

300s BCE
The Mauryan Empire takes control of the area.

1206
Muslims take control of Bengal.

1150
The Hindu Sena dynasty takes control of the region.

1608
Dhaka becomes the capital of the Mughal Empire's Bengal province.

ca. 1000 BCE
The Bang people settle in what is now Bangladesh.

750 CE
Buddhism comes to Bengal during the Pala dynasty.

1576
Bengal falls under the control of the Mughal Empire.

1757
The East India Company gains control of Bengal.

1857
People rise up against the East India Company in the Sepoy Mutiny.

1858
India becomes a crown colony.

1905–1912
Bengal is divided into East and West Bengal.

1952
Police kill student demonstrators in Dhaka during the Language Movement.

1947
India and Pakistan gain their independence.

| 2500 | BCE 0 CE | 1000 | 1250 | 1500 | 1600 | 1700 | 1800 | 1850 | 1900 | 1950 |

World History

ca. 2500 BCE
The Egyptians build the pyramids and the Sphinx in Giza.

ca. 563 BCE
The Buddha is born in India.

313 CE
The Roman emperor Constantine legalizes Christianity.

610
The Prophet Muhammad begins preaching a new religion called Islam.

1054
The Eastern (Orthodox) and Western (Roman Catholic) Churches break apart.

1095
The Crusades begin.

1215
King John seals the Magna Carta.

1300s
The Renaissance begins in Italy.

1347
The plague sweeps through Europe.

1453
Ottoman Turks capture Constantinople, conquering the Byzantine Empire.

1492
Columbus arrives in North America.

1500s
Reformers break away from the Catholic Church, and Protestantism is born.

1776
The U.S. Declaration of Independence is signed.

1789
The French Revolution begins.

1865
The American Civil War ends.

1879
The first practical lightbulb is invented.

1914
World War I begins.

1917
The Bolshevik Revolution brings communism to Russia.

1929
A worldwide economic depression begins.

1939
World War II begins.

1945
World War II ends.

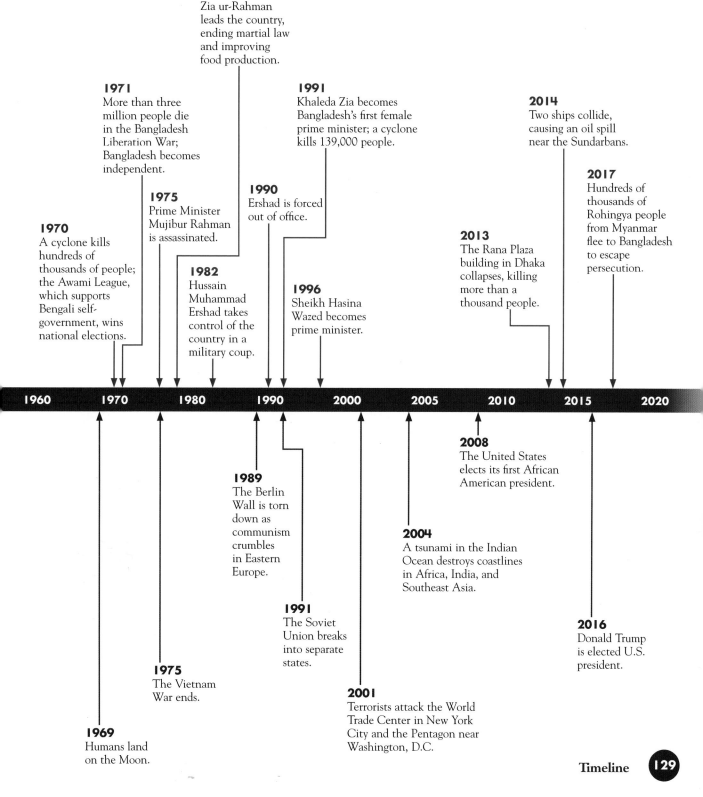

1975–1981
Zia ur-Rahman leads the country, ending martial law and improving food production.

1971
More than three million people die in the Bangladesh Liberation War; Bangladesh becomes independent.

1975
Prime Minister Mujibur Rahman is assassinated.

1970
A cyclone kills hundreds of thousands of people; the Awami League, which supports Bengali self-government, wins national elections.

1982
Hussain Muhammad Ershad takes control of the country in a military coup.

1990
Ershad is forced out of office.

1991
Khaleda Zia becomes Bangladesh's first female prime minister; a cyclone kills 139,000 people.

1996
Sheikh Hasina Wazed becomes prime minister.

2013
The Rana Plaza building in Dhaka collapses, killing more than a thousand people.

2014
Two ships collide, causing an oil spill near the Sundarbans.

2017
Hundreds of thousands of Rohingya people from Myanmar flee to Bangladesh to escape persecution.

| 1960 | 1970 | 1980 | 1990 | 2000 | 2005 | 2010 | 2015 | 2020 |

1989
The Berlin Wall is torn down as communism crumbles in Eastern Europe.

1991
The Soviet Union breaks into separate states.

2008
The United States elects its first African American president.

2004
A tsunami in the Indian Ocean destroys coastlines in Africa, India, and Southeast Asia.

2016
Donald Trump is elected U.S. president.

1975
The Vietnam War ends.

2001
Terrorists attack the World Trade Center in New York City and the Pentagon near Washington, D.C.

1969
Humans land on the Moon.

Fast Facts

Official name:	People's Republic of Bangladesh
Capital:	Dhaka
Official language:	Bengali
Official religion:	Islam
Year of founding:	1971
National anthem:	"Amar Shonar Bangla" ("My Golden Bengal")
Type of government:	Parliamentary democracy
Head of state:	President
Head of government:	Prime minister

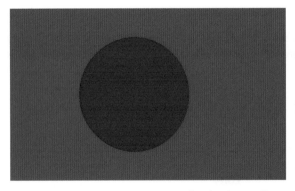

Left to right: **National flag, presidential guard**

Chittagong Hills

Area:	57,320 square miles (148,460 sq km)
Latitude and longitude:	24° N, 90° E
Bordering countries:	India to the west, north, and east; Myanmar to the southeast
Highest elevation:	Mount Keokradong, 4,035 feet (1,230 m)
Lowest elevation:	Sea level along the coast
Average daily high temperature:	In Dhaka, 91°F (33°C) in June, 80°F (27°C) in December
Average daily low temperature:	In Dhaka, 80°F (27°C) in June, 57°F (14°C) in December
Average annual precipitation:	In Dhaka, 85 inches (216 cm)

National population (2017 est.):	164,669,751	
Population of major cities (2018 est.):	Dhaka	10,356,500
	Chittagong	3,920,222
	Khulna	1,342,339
	Rajshahi	700,133
	Comilla	389,411

Landmarks:
- ▶ *Bangladesh National Museum*, Dhaka
- ▶ *Cox's Bazar beach*
- ▶ *National Martyrs' Memorial*, Dhaka
- ▶ *Sundarbans*, Bay of Bengal

Economy: Bangladesh is primarily agricultural. The main crops are rice, jute, and tea. Industry has grown quickly in recent years. Bangladesh now has one of the world's largest garment industries. Leather production has also increased. Traditional handicrafts like decorated pottery and woven baskets are made in Bangladesh and shipped throughout the world.

Currency: The taka. In 2018, $1 equaled 83 taka.

System of weights and measures: Metric system

Literacy rate: 72.8%

Common Bengali words and phrases:	*Hae/Jee*	Yes
	Na/Jee na	No
	Dhonno-baad	Thank you
	Nomoshkar	Hello/Good-bye
	Kemon achhen?	How are you?
	Bhaalo ache.	I am fine.
	Apnar naam kee?	What is your name?
	Amar naam . . .	My name is . . .
	Buj-tey paarchhi na	I don't understand.
	Maaf ko-roon/Khoma ko-roon	Sorry

Prominent Bangladeshis:

Sara Hossain (?–)
Supreme Court justice and human rights lawyer

Mujibur Rahman (1920–1975)
Father of Bangladesh

Rabindranath Tagore (1861–1941)
Nobel Prize–winning poet

Sheikh Hasina Wazed (1947–)
Prime minister

Muhammad Yunus (1940–)
Economist and winner of the Nobel Peace Prize

Clockwise from top: **Currency, Sheikh Hasina Wazed, schoolchildren**

To Find Out More

Books

▶ Perkins, Mitali. *Rickshaw Girl*. Watertown, MA: Charlesbridge, 2011.

▶ Perkins, Mitali. *Tiger Boy*. Watertown, MA: Charlesbridge, 2015.

▶ Yoo, Paula. *Twenty-Two Cents: Muhammad Yunus and the Village Bank*. New York: Lee & Low Books, 2014.

Video

▶ *Globe Trekker: Bangladesh*. London: Pilot Productions, 2012.

▶ *Years of Living Dangerously*. Episode 8. New York: Filmrise, 2014.

▶ Visit this Scholastic website for more information on Bangladesh: **www.factsfornow.scholastic.com** Enter the keyword **Bangladesh**

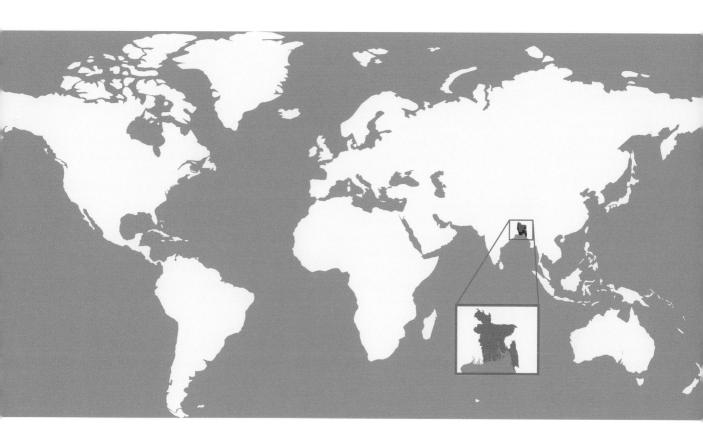

Index

Page numbers in *italics* indicate illustrations.

Meet the Author

TAMRA ORR IS THE AUTHOR OF MORE THAN 500 BOOKS FOR readers of all ages. She also writes many state and national tests for students in kindergarten through high school. Orr lives in the Pacific Northwest with her family and spends any free time she can find reading her endless pile of books and writing letters to people all over the world. A graduate of Ball State University, Orr loves to learn about places around the world and find out what makes each one unique. Her research process is a mixture of visiting hundreds of websites, as well as accessing local library resources and bookstores (she lives in the same city as the largest private bookstore in the world. They know her by sight!). Orr also conducts telephone and email interviews with a variety of experts. Orr has written books about many places in the United States, and also books about Turkey, Qatar, Indonesia, Slovenia, and many other countries. She hopes that when she eventually retires, she might get the chance to travel the world and visit all of these countries in person.

Photo Credits